Majestic

MIDDLE

TENNESSEE

Reid Smith

PELICAN PUBLISHING COMPANY

GRETNA 1998

This Book Is Humbly Dedicated

FIRST:

To the Dear Lord in Heaven,
Who not only supplied the thoughts,
Steadied my hand
And entered my heart during its
Writing,
But Who also saw to bread
On our table while this effort
Was being made

AND TO:

Mrs. Reuben Algood, a dear friend,
Whose boundless enthusiasm,
Countless hours of effort
And endless storehouse of knowl-
edge,
Not only helped make this book
A reality—
But also enabled the author
To come to know and love
Middle Tennessee almost as much
As she does.

****

Credit for the excellent watercolors illustrating the Introduction and the Battles of Franklin and Nashville belongs to Bob Gray, a young Alabamian whose keen awareness of what this book is all about could not help but flow through the talented tip of his brush. Without Bob's efforts MAJESTIC MIDDLE TENNESSEE would not be the same.

****

Library of Congress Cataloging in Publication Data

Smith, Reid.
  Majestic Middle Tennessee.

  Reprint. Originally published: Prattville, Ala:
Paddle Wheel Publications, c1975
    1. Historic buildings—Tennessee, Middle—Guide-books.
2. Dwellings—Tennessee, Middle—Guide-books. 3. Architecture,
Domestic—Tennessee, Middle—Guide-books. 4. Tennessee,
Middle—Description and travel—Guide-books. I. Title.
[F442.2.S64 1983]   917.68   8313328
ISBN 0-88289-121-9

First printing, 1975
First Pelican printing, 1982
Third printing, 1983
Fourth printing, 1990
Fifth printing, 1998

Printed in China

Acknowledgments
and
Contents

A special expression of gratitude goes to Mr. and Mrs. John Blair Jackson of Columbia for introducing the author to Majestic Middle Tennessee in the first place—to the members of the Maury County Historical Association and local chapter of the Association for the Preservation of Tennessee Antiquities who met together for endless hours to discuss the potential of this book and never gave up hope along the way—and finally, for the generous hospitality and enthusiasm of those owners of the historic old places that inspired this book:

Welcome
To

MAJESTIC MIDDLE

TENNESSEE! Here you will hear the heartbeat of

history thunder through distant hills and echo through hollows where Time walks with silent footsteps. In this place the scarlet and gold flames of fall will seem to deceive your very eyes. Out of this earth the tender green shoots of spring may somehow implant themselves within the deepest reaches of your soul.

Here the great Andrew Jackson lived and loved his dear Rachel and bowed his proud head above her grave. From this place Knox Polk climbed out of the shadows of obscurity and into the presidential chair.

Here Davy Crockett stalked knoll and glade with the same restless strides that marched him to the Alamo and into the Halls of Glory. Perched on the knuckles of these hills, young Matt Maury pondered the mysteries of the Seven Seas and charted his way into the heart of every sailor who has ever dared sail them since.

Here, within the staunch muzzle of these valleys, John Bell Hood—a stiff-armed, one-legged memory of a man—wrote one of the bloodiest pages in American history, when never did so many die for so little in such a short time.

There lingers, too, in this place the ever green memory of a humble slave who once pledged his life three times to the end of a British rope and lived to walk away with the King's own medal for his unfailing loyalty to his master.

In our own time, just as New Orleans gave birth to "The Blues", the hardy hand of these hills would rock the Cradle of Country Music until it grew into manhood as the world-renowned "Nashville Sound".

Welcome you are to MAJESTIC MIDDLE TENNESSEE! Among these hills you can hear the sands of the ages softly covering the tracks of the past. As you stand listening, off in the blue spray of distance some grand stallion may hoist his head to sniff the sweet scent of Man and Nature walking together. In this place there is the strange feeling—that, while stone walls and rail fences seem to wander aimlessly against the sky, they always somehow inevitably point toward the very altar of God.

7

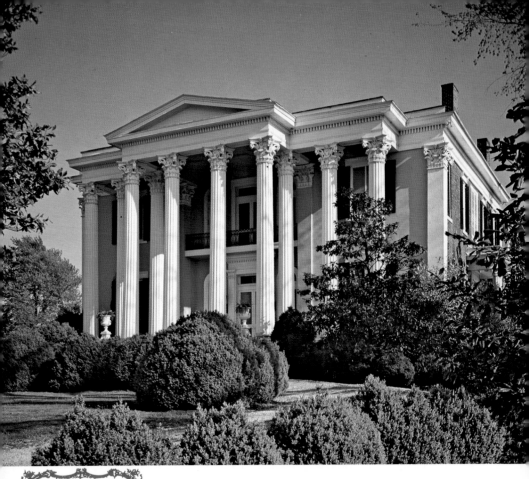

RATTLE AND SNAP
1845
Ten tall pillars and a game of "beans"

"Magnificent" has to be the first word in any description of RATTLE AND SNAP. Though not the firstborn of the long line of Polk mansions to march across the Maury County countryside, RATTLE AND SNAP remains today far and away the crown prince of them all.

Conceived in the womb of a sincere love of sheer beauty, and nurtured in the lap of an age that could afford it, RATTLE AND SNAP stands in elegant tribute to that time long past when a craftsman's pride matched the might of his master's purse.

Though the great stone foundation of RATTLE AND SNAP is sunk deep in the loamy bosom of Middle Tennessee's heartland, the roots of its real beginnings and unique name reach all the way back to post-Revolutionary North Carolina and a bag of lowly beans.

If not a great deal is known about Col. William Polk, the proof is in the pudding that he had, at least, three obvious talents—siring exceptional sons, buying up Revolutionary land grants from fellow veterans, and emerging victorious from a game of "beans" with the Governor of North Carolina's deed for 5,648 prime Maury County acres tucked neatly in his pocket. To this particular tract lying along the Columbia-Mt. Pleasant Pike the good Colonel attached a very appropriate and colorful sobriquet, RATTLE AND SNAP.

8

When William Polk divided his RATTLE AND SNAP holdings among four of his sons—Lucius J., Leonidas, Rufus K., and George W. Polk—the latter, George, decided to retain the original name for his portion of his father's estate.

After choosing for the site of his future mansion the brow of a commanding hillock deep within a dense woodland of giant oak, black walnut, and towering elm, George Polk purchased an additional 800 acres to the eastward of his RATTLE AND SNAP properties. Here he built "The Cottage," a nine-room, one-story, "unpretentious" frame house. Within these walls would be born all but one of George and Sally Hilliard Polk's children. The Polks were still living at "The Cottage" in the early 1840's when work was soon begun on what their slaves soon came to refer to as "The Big House."

Never a man of half measures, George Polk seems to have been determined from the very beginning that RATTLE AND SNAP plantation would be as self-sustaining as possi-

RATTLE AND SNAP has it all. This intricate ironwork has been blended ever so carefully with every last detail of this magnificent Greek Revival house.

ble. To his own forests, he looked for the massive framing timbers that would span the walls built of brick fired in his own kilns. Upon his own shoulders, George Polk placed the burden of overseeing the workmanship, furnished almost entirely by his own skilled masons and carpenters.

Even as ground was being broken, George Polk—ever planning ahead—had sent across the wide Atlantic for the German landscape artist whose charge it would be to plan the winding walks, plant the many-acred lawns, vegetable and flower gardens, and beds of evergreen. All—from the five huge cisterns for watering the grounds to the three extensive greenhouses that would yield everything from violets to bananas—must stand in readiness at RATTLE AND SNAP'S completion. For Master Polk's "open house" his German gardener must see not only to turnips on the table but also that his herb beds sprouted spices like sage, thyme, and horseradish, and brought forth such early day medicinals as horehound, catnip flax and rhubarb.

Even this vast domain of such abundance had certain limits, however. To Italy George Polk was forced to turn for RATTLE AND SNAP'S exquisite marble mantels, while the great twenty-six foot Corinthian columns for the front veranda had to be shipped in sections from distant Cincinnati. They were first boated down the Ohio, thence up the Cumberland to Nashville, and, finally, ox-carted overland to the Polk plantation. In years to come, as the blue tide of the Federal army swept up from the southward, the smallest of George Polk's sons would lower the family silver into the hollow sanctuary of one of these mighty pillars.

Forever an outstanding feature of RATTLE AND SNAP'S outer grace and constant beauty, the grillwork of the east portico may well have been cast in the iron foundries of Pittsburgh, and yet there is an intricate delicacy here that suggests the Creole flavor of far New Orleans.

So sophisticated and perfect too are RATTLE AND SNAP'S interior cornices and ceiling

9

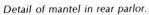

The Italian marble mantels in
RATTLE AND SNAP are some of
the most beautiful in the
entire South.

The dining room at RATTLE AND
SNAP is crowned with an exquisite
Waterford chandelier.

A bed fit for a princess.

medallions, there arises the distinct conviction that here, once again, George Polk was forced to thrust aside his pride and look beyond even his own bountiful realm for such meticulous care and dedicated artisanship.

Sometime in 1845, while cousin James Knox Polk was still warming the presidential chair in Washington, George Polk moved his family into magnificent RATTLE AND SNAP—a house that would stand in long tribute, not only to the mind that conceived it, but also to the skilled hands and constant pride that wove a man's dreams into a peerless reality of his age.

Pitcher and tea service hidden in columns of RATTLE AND SNAP during Federal invasion of Maury County.

11

CLIFTON PLACE
1839
Within the year—an amazing feat

CLIFTON PLACE, just off the Columbia-Mt. Pleasant Pike, was the first of Maury County's great Pillow houses. It was the home of a famous Middle Tennessee soldier whose star would rise in one war and set in another he was too old to fight. This man was Gen. Gideon J. Pillow, graduate of West Point, a hero of the Mexican War and second in command of one of the Southern Confederacy's first military disasters.

If the first Gideon Pillow in Maury County was of raw and unhoned pioneer stock, his son and namesake had been reared a fine gentleman with a fine gentleman's taste for a magnificent Greek Revival house like CLIFTON PLACE. With a pocketbook that could afford for him to leave nothing to chance, young Gideon Pillow contracted with Maury County's master builder, the one and only Nathan Vaught, to see to every last classic detail.

Even though CLIFTON PLACE was raised under the hand of one so skilled in his craft as Nathan Vaught it is an amazing feat that such a house, along with its two story brick kitchen and servants' quarters, was completed within the unbelievably short span of a single year. Enormous in its classical proportions and housing twelve rooms and two huge halls, CLIFTON PLACE, according to Vaught's own diary, was begun in 1838 and finished inside and out by early '39.

Almost all of the materials for Gideon Pillow's home were literally wrested from the good earth of the General's own properties. The tons of stone that went into the foundation, floored the front portico and supplied bases for the four massive Ionic columns was quarried on the premises. The clay for the thousands upon thousands of slave-made bricks that gird CLIFTON PLACE'S regally parapeted walls was dug from the brawny shoulders of its rolling acres. Even the wild cherry, planed into doors, shaped into molding and carved into mantels, was a native product of Gideon Pillow's vast domain. Perhaps little more than the main house's sprawling tin roof, the cast balustrade of the entrance's overhanging balcony and certain interior hardware had to be imported from the world beyond.

If majestic old CLIFTON PLACE could speak to us today, it might have a great deal to say about its first and most famous lord and master. Perhaps it would recall a young and handsome Gideon Pillow galloping off to fight in the war with Mexico, a straight-backed and proud Gideon Pillow on his triumphal return as a lean-shanked hero of those glorious days of youth and abundance. Among its memories would also be an older Gideon Pillow, somewhat stooped now and teary-eyed at the honor of being chosen to command Tennessee's troops at the outset of the Civil War. Less blissfully could CLIFTON PLACE recall a bitter and disillusioned Gideon Pillow, bent even more now with the blame for his part in the Southern defeat at Fort Donelson. Sadly it can remember a broken and disgraced Gideon Pillow who scrawled his name in disgust on his resignation from the Army of the Confederacy. Proudly this old place could remind us, too, of a Gideon Pillow who, even after all of this, buckled on his sword—swallowed his wounded pride—and led a gallant charge at the Battle of Murfreesboro to wipe away the tarnish from his name.

If the Civil War cost Gen. Pillow some anxious moments about his reputation, before it was done it would also cost him ". . . 409 negroes, 4 gin houses, valued at $10,000 each; 10,000 pounds of bacon; 2,000 hogs; 500 head of cattle; and 2,000 bales of cotton . . ." The cotton was burned by the Confederates to keep it from falling into the hands of the Federals who looted and pillaged CLIFTON PLACE more than once as the home of a Rebel general.

BETHEL PLACE

1855

The third in a lordly line

BETHEL PLACE is a typical Pillow house—pure Greek Revival and grand in every sense of the word.

This fine old home was built in 1855 for Jerome Pillow by that master artisan of Middle Tennessee, Nathan Vaught. Jerome was the youngest brother of Gen. Gideon and Granville Pillow, who had already given Maury County CLIFTON PLACE and PILLOW PLACE.

As a brother-in-law of Edward W. Dale, Nathan Vaught was a remote kinsman of Jerome Pillow. Mr. Dale's daughter, Elvira, had given her hand in marriage to Jerome some years before ground was broken for BETHEL PLACE.

Just as there must have been marked similarities among the three Pillow boys, Jerome's home would bear a distinct resemblance to the elegant antebellum manor houses of his two older brothers. BETHEL PLACE would be trademarked by the same towering Ionic columns and acute attention to classic detail. Like Gideon's CLIFTON PLACE, a handsomely pedimented portico would lead into a spacious two story interior where life was meant to be lived and enjoyed in the full abundance of the plantation South.

To the rear of BETHEL PLACE, Nathan Vaught stationed the typical dependencies of that day and time—the brick servants' quarters, outkitchen, carriage house and the family stables. The quaint little Gothic-flavored building to the east of "the big house" is said to have been built years ago as a law office. BETHEL PLACE'S stone wall is typical Middle Tennessee, while the great cast iron gate opening into its immediate grounds may well be one of the most beautiful in the whole state.

During the Civil War a number of sharp skirmishes took place around Jerome Pillow's house. One of his own sons, young Edward L. Pillow, had run off at fifteen to fight with the First Tennessee Cavalry and lived to die of old age in Helena, Ark. Oddly enough, it would be a son-in-law and another Rebel soldier, Capt. William Decatur Bethel, who would furnish this old house the name by which it has been known for generations of Pillow descendants who have always made BETHEL PLACE their home.

ST. JOHN'S EPISCOPAL CHURCH

1842

A child of Man and the altar of God

Of all the landmarks strewn up and down the Columbia-Mt. Pleasant Pike, none is more beloved than historic old ST. JOHN'S CHURCH.

Long venerated as the final resting place of Tennessee's first Episcopal Bishop, the Rt. Reverend James H. Otey, ST. JOHN'S was the inspiration of another famous man of The Cloth, Leonidas Polk—"Bishop-General of the Confederacy."

A graduate of West Point and future Bishop of the Diocese of Louisiana, this son of paradox in 1839 prevailed on his three brothers—Lucius, Rufus and George—and

Acorn column capital from
ASHWOOD HALL, once the home
of Bishop Leonidas Polk—one of the
founders of historic ST. JOHN'S
EPISCOPAL CHURCH on the
Columbia-Mt. Pleasant Pike.

a half-brother, William J. Polk, to join him in building a suitable house of worship for their families and those of their neighbors in the surrounding community. Three years later the devout generosity of these five sons of old Col. William Polk was blessed with the consecration of ST. JOHN'S by Bishop Otey on Sept. 4, 1842.

At each of their deaths all of the Polk boys, except Leonidas, would be laid to rest in the churchyard alongside Bishop Otey and two other Bishops of Tennessee—Maxon and Barth.

Gothic in concept and crowned with the natural beauty of its Middle Tennessee woodlands, ST. JOHN'S EPISCOPAL CHURCH saw the Civil War plant the feet of foe and friend alike on its doorstep. On their way to help Grant fight the Battle of Shiloh in the spring of '62, Don Carlos Buell's Yankees stopped off here just long enough to carry off several of ST. JOHN'S handsome organ pipes as souvenirs. Two years hence that hard-hitting Rebel general from Arkansas, Pat Cleburne, would pause beyond the stone fences of this old church to remark: "So this is the church built by Gen. Leonidas Polk and members of his family? If I am killed in the impending battle, I request that my body be laid to rest in this, the most beautiful and peaceful spot I ever beheld." In a matter of days this same Pat Cleburne and two fellow generals of the Confederacy—H. B. Granbury and O. F. Strahl—all three shot to death at Franklin, would lie in temporary graves on the grounds of ST. JOHN'S.

Several months earlier a sudden salvo of Sherman's cannon had killed Bishop-General Polk on the slanting slopes of faraway Pine Mountain, Ga. President Davis had mourned at the time that not since Stonewall Jackson's death had the South suffered such "an irreparable loss."

Interior of ST. JOHN'S. At the rear of the sanctuary is the original slave balcony.

HAMILTON PLACE
1832
To the White House for a bride

It was the role of HAMILTON PLACE to be the first of the great Polk mansions to raise their majestic pillars along the Columbia-Mt. Pleasant Pike. Built in 1832 by Lucius Polk—third son of that enterprising old Revolutionary veteran and Middle Tennessee land baron, Col. William Polk—HAMILTON PLACE would be named in memory of a brother, who had died earlier at Yale while yet in his twentieth year.

If Lucius Polk had put the cart before the horse by building his homeplace before he had a wife, his heart had settled long ago on pretty Mary Jane Eastin, a beguiling and favorite niece of none other than Mrs. Andrew Jackson, the first mistress of THE HERMITAGE. There were, though, certain complications that had to be overcome before HAMILTON PLACE would have its own first lady.

With Rachel Jackson's death on the eve of her husband's first inauguration, Mary Jane had left Lucius Polk behind in Tennessee and traipsed off to Washington to assist her Aunt Emily Donelson in her new duties as "Uncle Andrew's" White House hostess.

Vivaciously attractive, Mary Jane Eastin had been quick to make her own waves in the capital city's social swirl, and Lucius Polk soon realized that persuading her to forsake the golden glitter of Washington for the foothills of Middle Tennessee would take some doing. However, with typical Polk resolution in the set of his jaw, he turned his back on HAMILTON PLACE and rode off to Washington City sometime in the early spring of 1832.

17

The Ham Table at HAMILTON PLACE would be the envy of most any collector of rare antiques.

On an April day of this very same year, with the President of the United States nodding his head in shaggy approval, Mary Jane Eastin became the White House bride of one Lucius Polk, "the boy back home from Tennessee."

During Lucius and Mary Polk's reign as master and mistress of HAMILTON PLACE, among the many notables to pass through the triple-arched splendor of its great entrance hall was cousin James Knox Polk, soon destined for the mantle of eleventh President of the United States. An even more frequent visitor was brother Leonidas Polk, first as a man of The Cloth and later as the famous "Fighting Bishop-General of the Confederacy."

Perhaps, too, it was beneath the grand medallion of HAMILTON PLACE'S central hallway that Col. Henry C. Yeatman asked for the hand of the Polks' second daughter, Mary.

At the death of Lucius and Mary Jane Polk, the Yeatmans fell heir to HAMILTON PLACE; and within these sturdy brick walls, each of their children and grandchildren were to be born. It was also at this same HAMILTON PLACE, on an October day, 1910, that Col. Yeatman would yield up his life in a strange quirk of fate. A survivor of the fierce fury of many a Civil War fight, the good Colonel—for a simple act of kindness—would be brought home to die in the fading twilight of a fall afternoon. A gallant attempt to save his faithful dog from the churning wheels of a local train had done what no enemy cannon had ever been able to do.

CHERRY GLEN
Before 1810
A bathtub and a Parisian palace

CHERRY GLEN has long been tied to the apron strings of Maury County history.

The original two room dogtrot portion of this old house on Mt. Pleasant Pike was built by Lucius Polk sometime before 1810. There is reason to believe that Lucius, the oldest of the Polk boys to settle in this section of Maury County, made this his log cabin home while he was building handsome HAMILTON PLACE nearby.

In 1858 CHERRY GLEN passed from the hand of the Polk family when it was bought by Col. Fount Wade, a son-in-law of colorful Gideon Pillow of CLIFTON PLACE.

Col. Wade hardly gave the beds a chance to be made before he began an extensive remodelling that would change the whole demeanor of his new home. First, CHERRY GLEN'S original dogtrot would be extended and enclosed into a central hallway of some thirty feet, off of which a door would open into the then rare convenience of an inside bathroom. Featured here would be the singular luxury of a copper-lined bathtub. Even though it had to be filled by hand, this tub was a source of amazement in that day and time since it could actually empty itself outside of the house. Another innovation of this 1858 renovation was the addition of a spacious dining hall. This would be adjoined by a dogtrotted outkitchen and cook's room at the rear. Despite these changes and additions, Col. Wade's crowning contribution to CHERRY GLEN was its east and west octagonal wings. Inspired by Louis XV's Petit Trianon in Paris,

The dining room at CHERRY GLEN was the inspiration of its second owner, Col. Daniel Fountain Wade.

these two eight-sided bedrooms would give CHERRY GLEN its own special place among the truly unique antebellum homes of Middle Tennessee.

During the Civil War a young Confederate scout, William H. Lipscomb, unable to make his way to his own home near Cross Bridges, once spent a night here in hiding from the Yankees. Years later William Lipscomb's grandniece, Annie Barton Armstrong, would be brought to CHERRY GLEN as a bride.

To the credit of a house so long associated with the growing pains of early Maury County, the Tennessee Historical Commission, in July, 1973, notified Mrs. Armstrong that CHERRY GLEN had been selected for the National Register of Historical Places in this country—a tribute well deserved by this grand old monument to the past.

The quaint little log house hovering at the rear of CHERRY GLEN dates back to the days when the Indians were still paying unwelcome visits on the early pioneer settlers of what is today Maury County.

MANOR HALL
1859
On a summer's night—a brutal attack

When Martin Luther Stockard built MANOR HALL in 1859, he gave to Mt. Pleasant the crown jewel of all its antebellum homes. With obvious pride in such an achievement, Mr. Stockard saw to it that his initials and MANOR HALL'S building date were branded forever near the tops of the two front chimneys that rear in towering splendor above the regal shoulders of this grand old place.

As a monument to an era when no pillar could rise too high, no ocean was too wide to cross for the very best of everything, and no purse was spared to bring both about, MANOR HALL crowns the crest of a spacious and gently rising lawn that seems to lift it curiously apart from the hustle and bustle of the present day world beyond. At the same time, its great bulk has a way of hiding from view the "old Quarters" and ancient smokehouse that still hover in traditional humility within their own long lost universe of salty timbers, fleeting shadows, and the empty cornucopia of the days that used to be.

If, in all its elegant grandeur, MANOR HALL signified a special triumph on the stage of Martin Luther Stockard's life; so, too, would this same MANOR HALL witness tragedy waiting in the wings of a hot June night, 1874. While strolling on his front lawn in the peace and quiet of an early summer's evening, Col. Stockard was suddenly and viciously attacked by an unknown assailant who left him for dead in the sultry darkness. Never fully recovering from this brutal assault, Martin Luther Stockard had but three short years left to him as MANOR HALL'S builder and first master.

Ironically, at Col. Stockard's death, title to MANOR HALL passed to one Rev. John Stephenson Frierson, for forty years the beloved pastor of Mt. Pleasant Presbyterian Church. As the founder and moving spirit of historic Hay Long College, this progenitor of MANOR HALL'S present owners had been originally the first white man ever to own the phosphate-rich acres upon which MANOR HALL stands today—long undisputed as the rarest treasure in all of antebellum Mt. Pleasant.

ZION CHURCH
1807-1813-1849
By the sweat of their faith

No early house of worship in Maury County can claim a richer heritage of lore and legend than old ZION CHURCH.

Between the frontier years of 1805 and 1808 a small group of Scottish-Irish Presbyterians turned their backs on their Kingstree, S.C., homeplace and set out for the heartlands of Middle Tennessee.

In 1807, the year Maury County was founded, these hardy South Carolinians purchased 5,120 acres of Gen. Nathanael Greene's Revolutionary land grant and set to work to establish a religious settlement that would come to be known as the Zion Community. Within a single week in August of this same year, true to their Calvinistic leanings and before building their own homes, this tiny little flock of devout pioneers raised the walls of a humble log meeting house that would serve as their place of worship for the next six years.

ZION CHURCH'S first pastor was the Rev. James White Stephenson, a veteran of the Revolution and former teacher of young Andrew Jackson in the Waxhaws. ZION CHURCH would later figure in the education of another future President—James Knox Polk.

The second ZION CHURCH, built of wood and brick, was completed in 1813 and was the focal point of religious life in this little community for some thirty-five highly fruitful years.

Front view of ZION CHURCH as seen from portion of old cemetery. Veterans of every major war in this nation's history are buried here.

The present building as we know it today was raised in 1849 out of the devoted sweat of slave and master alike, laboring side by side out of a mutual desire to serve a common God. All work and materials were supplied on the basis of what each member could afford to give. Three-storied and boasting a sanctuary of 4,000 square feet, its construction cost was a paltry $7,000.

It is an interesting sidelight that, even after the Civil War, ZION'S recently freed Negro congregation still continued to pack its slave galleries. At one point these black communicants actually outnumbered the families of their former masters. As late as 1867, despite the bitter winds of Reconstruction blowing their way, the white members of ZION CHURCH reorganized a Sabbath School for their black brothers in the Lord. They were rewarded in these efforts by the loyalty of old Riley Witherspoon, ZION'S last remaining Negro communicant. Riley lingered on as a faithful member, sitting alone Sunday after Sunday in the old slave gallery, long after the rest of his race had departed to build their own church.

Though never a bona fide communicant himself, "Uncle Andy" Brown's faithful service as sexton of ZION CHURCH spilled over into the second decade of this century. For almost a whole lifetime of Sabbaths, "Uncle Andy" had left two glasses of water on the pulpit for the preacher before striding proudly up the aisle to his place in the choir loft to pump away on ZION'S old Pilcher Pipe organ.

The earliest grave in ZION CHURCH'S historic cemetery belongs to Robert Frierson, dead just two months after his religious leanings had led him into early Maury County. Sleeping nearby are fifteen Revolutionary veterans, three soldiers of the War of 1812, one who saw service against the Seminoles in 1836, some sixty fighting sons of the Confederacy and the dead from two World Wars. Lying here also in quiet anticipation, awaiting the glorious blast of Gabriel's Horn, are twelve ministers of the Gospel and thirteen of their earthly consorts in the Faith.

For the babies who have been baptized here—the children who found their first Easter egg here—for the young brides and grooms wedded here—the families who have worshipped and been buried here—old ZION CHURCH will always have a special place in the hearts of them all.

Monument to loyal slaves of early Zion settlers. "Daddy Ben" chose to face the gallows rather than betray his master to the British, and lived to walk away from the gibbet with the medal of their admiration.

23

OLD MAYES PLACE

After 1811

Eight generations long

When the old Zion Colony of Presbyterians began moving into Maury County around 1805, it brought along its own physician. He was Dr. Samuel Mayes, a Revolutionary veteran under Gen. Nathanael Greene and a graduate of the University of Pennsylvania Medical School.

If Dr. Mayes was a humble man, dedicated to the service of his fellowmen, he also built a humble house to serve his early frontier needs. Its crude log walls raised in 1808, the good doctor's cabin had the good fortune of being completely restored sometime in 1925. Hovering in the shadow of the home that for generations has been known by Maury Countians as the OLD MAYES PLACE, this demure little conversation piece now serves the present family as a quaintly charming guest house that will be long remembered by those fortunate enough to enjoy its simple hospitality.

Just when the OLD MAYES PLACE itself was actually built is rather vague. Some say that it was the handiwork of his widow sometime shortly after Dr. Mayes' death in 1811. Others give the credit to a son, George Whitfield Mayes, and place the date as late as 1855.

It was George Mayes' beautiful daughter, Jennie, who married Samuel Rush Watkins, author of those ever colorful Civil War memoirs, "Company Aytch or the Adventures of a High Private."

So far, eight generations of descendants of Ophelia Mayes Orr, a sister of Jennie Watkins, have run and romped across the deeply shaded lawns of this fine old Maury County homeplace. Perhaps this will go on forever.

MULBERRY HILL
Circa 1828
Death on the front steps

MULBERRY HILL is an old house that can remember the festive joy of life abundant. It can also recall the bursting bubbles of fortunes made and lost overnight.

Standing well manicured and tall on a portion of what was once Gen. Nathanael Greene's 25,000 acre Revolutionary land grant, MULBERRY HILL was built sometime around 1828 by Royal Ferguson, a pioneer in Middle Tennessee's early pig iron industry. As sole owner and operator of the old Mt. Jasper Furnace in Wayne County, Mr. Ferguson would taste briefly the sweet milk of sudden success. For nearly a decade MULBERRY HILL reflected this prosperity with sumptuous strawberry feasts, handsome levees and gala soirees.

Just what part the Panic of 1837 played in Royal Ferguson's sudden misfortunes, we cannot be sure. It is a matter of record, however, that he lost MULBERRY HILL in the early summer of the following year and died two months later.

Edward W. Dale, another iron man and MULBERRY HILL'S second master, fared even worse. Financial reverses, legend says, caused Mr. Dale to take his own life here on July 7, 1840.

MULBERRY HILL'S third owner, prominent Matthew Delamere Cooper, produced numerous improvements on the original house under the skillful eye of Maury County's master builder, Nathan Vaught. Mr. Cooper also produced an outstanding son.

The Civil War had hardly begun before dashing Duncan Brown Cooper found himself a nineteen-year-old colonel of Confederate guerilla fighters. Before the War's end "Dunc" Cooper would be praised and held in awe throughout the South.

Family legend says that when another Cooper son, also in the Confederate service, was followed home one night by an unknown Federal trooper, the Yankee was mysteriously shot to death on the front steps of MULBERRY HILL.

LIBERTY HALL
1844
He bet bales on a "dark horse"

Thanks to a man with a plentiful pocketbook and the courage of his convictions, Maury County has a house like LIBERTY HALL.

Built in 1844 by George Pope Webster as the hub of a 1,200 acre Middle Tennessee plantation, LIBERTY HALL has been one of the undisputed antebellum landmarks of Maury's Cross Bridges Community for more than 130 years. L-shaped, with a careful blending of Georgian with the white-pillared flair for classic pretention, this old house's heritage of longevity was assured through a tastefully devoted restoration that began in 1966. When the John O. Dillinghams undertook this monumental task, their cardinal rule was a minimum of change and a maximum of effort to preserve for coming generations the original and varied charms of LIBERTY HALL. There is no better place to look for the proof of their success than in the pudding of this heirloom of the past so handsomely preserved for the future.

Fourteen-inch walls of slave-made brick guard the regal interior of this fine old house. As a further safeguard against the ever present danger of fire, the old kitchen at the rear of the house was set apart and connected to the main body by the traditional breezeway. Below ground LIBERTY HALL boasts an ancient wine cellar and two additional antebellum-style utility rooms. Strung overhead are the hand hewn sills that have defied termite and time to recall those days of virgin forests and hard-muscled pride of workmanship.

The two-storied world of LIBERTY HALL is one of countless splendors, ranging from the wavy nostalgia of hand-rolled windowpanes to the graceful slant of a solid cherry railing for the stairway of the main entrance hall. Its floors planked in everlasting ash, its rooms graced by moldings turned under the hand of a master craftsman, LIBERTY HALL'S interior bespeaks a mellow grandeur all its own. Outside, its crowning legacy of the long gone life of true leisure is found in this old place's numerous porches, brick terraces, and endlessly wandering lawns.

As an early Middle Tennessean of the planter class, the builder of LIBERTY HALL, George Pope Webster, could hardly be expected to be less than a dyed-in-the-pocket-book Democrat. When his Maury County neighbor, James Knox Polk, America's first "dark horse" candidate, flung his hat into the Presidential ring, Mr. Webster published the courage of his convictions in the local newspaper for all of his good Whig friends to see: "1,000 on the general result, in money or its equivalent, one bale of cotton on each state from Maine to Louisiana. Now, ye coons, dance up to either of the above propositions.   G. P. Webster, Oct. 16, 1844"

LIPSCOMB PLACE
Late 1830's
The hearth of champions

The LIPSCOMB PLACE, snuggled in a picturesque valley near Cross Bridges, is as Middle Tennessee as sour mash whiskey, smoked ham and the fine horseflesh that has made this old Bigby Creek plantation famous.

Begun in the late 1830's by Maj. George Lipscomb, a veteran of Jackson's Florida campaigns, this early Maury County hearthstone was once the home of the celebrated stallion, McMeen's Traveler. As an ancestor of Star Pointer, the first harness pacer in history to break the two-minute mile, Traveler was also the sire of a colt that would gain fame right after the Civil War as the proud Prince Pulaski.

When the closing months of the War brought Yankee raiders galloping over the hill toward the LIPSCOMB PLACE, both Traveler and his three-year-old son, the future Prince, were confiscated from Maj. Lipscomb.

Unfortunately, Traveler would die of old age by the time the Union Army reached Shelbyville. After the southern surrender, when all captured livestock was sold at the Federal contraband corral in Nashville, his thoroughbred son was bought by a Maj. Allman of Marshall County. To the Major belongs the credit for developing this half-starved young stallion into the famous Prince Pulaski.

By the time he was sold to a group of Maury Countians in 1870, the Prince had ". . .taken more premiums . . ." than any horse in his class in all of Tennessee.

Five years of defeat and Reconstruction had been less kind to Maj. Lipscomb, now forced by finances to stable and board the very horse he had once owned. Even more pitifully ironic were the size of his fees: $5 for the season and a pasturage charge of fifty cents a week.

A happier note was added to the story of the old LIPSCOMB PLACE more recently, however, when another of its fine thoroughbreds, Ebony's Miss Blaze, won the World Championship in the Yearling Class at Shelbyville's 1974 Walking Horse Celebration.

One of the distinct charms of the LIPSCOMB PLACE is that it has been touched only lightly by the fingertips of time and change. What has been added or altered with the passing years has been so subtly and tastefully done that this old house is much the same as it was when it sent three of Maj. Lipscomb's young sons off to fight for the Confederacy more than a century ago.

VINE HILL
Circa 1836
"On a clear day you can see forever"

Although there is no pretension toward elegance in the lavish sense, VINE HILL is an outstanding example of the grand early Middle Tennessee farmhouse.

Gleaming flawlessly and iced in resplendent white like a giant birthday cake, this old house is mounted upon one of the most commanding knuckles of Maury County's Highland Rim. Raised to these heights around 1836 by James Henry Webster, VINE HILL'S view of the sprawling miles between Cross Bridges and the Hampshire Pike is truly a sight to behold. On a clear day even parts of four surrounding counties—Giles, Lawrence, Lewis and Hickman—are clearly visible in the distance.

As late as 1963 VINE HILL was rescued from the brink of oblivion, when Mrs. Charles Deere Wiman, a great-granddaughter of its builder, undertook a massive restoration of this old house. When the monumental task of reclaiming VINE HILL from the waifs of abandonment and neglect was finally completed, it was presented by Mrs. Wiman to the Maury County Historical Society in 1971 to be preserved as a permanent head-quarters open to tours authorized and supervised by the Society.

With its upper and lower Great Halls each measuring a generous sixteen by sixty feet and high of ceiling in the typical tradition of a working plantation manor house, VINE HILL boasts certain innovations that make this old place unique unto itself. Stairways located at either end of the cross halls provide a double access to and from the second story. None can deny that this was a very farsighted arrangement in a day and time when fire was an ever present hazard of plantation living. Another interesting feature of VINE HILL'S interior is the convenience of originally built-in closets in each of its bedrooms and in the library, a trait rarely found in Middle Tennessee homes of this early vintage.

One of the added charms of VINE HILL today is that this old Maury County homestead is still surrounded by most of its original dependencies. Out back is the quaint and traditionally detached kitchen, completely restored to its former usefulness. The present guest house was once a portion of the early slave quarters, while, gouged out of the hill nearby and still intact, is one of this section's few remaining ice houses. At the rear of the house, next to the kitchen, VINE HILL'S original farm bell hangs poised in its cast iron cradle as if waiting to ring back those long gone better days of yesteryear.

JONATHAN WEBSTER HOME
1808-1826
Mule man of Big Bigby Creek

With little more than a pocketknife and a few jackasses, Jonathan Webster managed to carve out for himself one of the earliest fortunes in Maury County.

This enterprising Revolutionary veteran is believed to have plodded into the wilds of Middle Tennessee from Georgia sometime before 1808.

With his sleeves rolled up to the elbow of typical frontier optimism, Jonathan Webster sowed the seeds of his first prosperity by hacking out the logs of a little gristmill on Big Bigby Creek, west of Columbia and near Cross Bridges.

These were the days when local farmers looked to teams of oxen to wrench out the stumps and clear the land. Jonathan Webster must have found new favor with his neighbors when he introduced a number of jackasses into the community and saw to it that these sluggish oxen were soon replaced by far more efficient teams of sturdy Maury County mules.

By 1808 enough prosperity had knocked at Jonathan Webster's door for him to build the three rear rooms of the house that was the first brick residence in this section of Maury County. According to the National Archives in Washington, the two story front section was not added until 1826.

Though not fine when measured on the yardstick of the white-pillared planter age yet to come, Mr. Webster's brick house on the hill must have afforded him a special station in these parts, when many of his neighbors were still mighty proud of four log walls and a dirt floor, swept smooth by a cornshuck broom.

If Jonathan Webster's jackasses had made an important contribution to Maury County's mule population, two wives would furnish Mr. Webster with a handsome brood of eleven children. A pair of his sons would grow up to cut their own initials on the antebellum panorama of majestic Middle Tennessee. Around 1836 James would crown a nearby crest with the noble profile of VINE HILL. Eight years later his brother, George Pope Webster, would add the final flourish of splendor to regal old LIBERTY HALL.

29

KENNEDY PLACE
1840-1856
A generous gift to an adopted son

When it comes to architecture, Middle Tennessee has it all.

The KENNEDY PLACE, on Maury County's Williamsport Pike, is one of the finest examples of the 'piano box' house to be found anywhere. With its recessed front veranda and projected flanking wings, this old home can claim a distinct kinship to the famous WIGWAM in Natchez.

The oldest five room portion of the KENNEDY PLACE dates to around 1840 and was built by Robert H. Jennings. Nine years later Jennings sold this house and a hundred prime Middle Tennessee acres to William E. Kennedy for $1800.

A distinguished Maury Countian, John Bell Hamilton, is credited with creating the KENNEDY PLACE'S 'piano box' effect, when he added the bedroom wings after purchasing the house in 1856. At the time of the sale Hamilton's deed contained the rather unusual provision that ". . . Kennedy may retain possession of the west rooms, kitchen, smoke house and such cribs and servant houses as he cannot conveniently vacate, until the 1st of March next . . ."

The third master of the KENNEDY PLACE was a versatile man who could boast many accomplishments during the span of his eighty years. He was a prosperous planter, held numerous public offices, was an active Methodist minister and served as a Captain in the First Tennessee Confederate Cavalry, along with his adopted son, Thomas Hamilton Williams.

Since John Bell Hamilton outlived his wife and had no surviving children, the KENNEDY PLACE came down to Thomas Williams at Mr. Hamilton's death in 1887.

As a grandson of the founder and namesake of nearby Williamsport, Thomas Hamilton Williams would live to make his own waves in postwar Middle Tennessee. Turning to the most modern farming methods of his day, he soon transformed the KENNEDY PLACE into one of the most progressive plantations in this section of the state. His Oak Spring Creamery, which shipped fresh milk as far away as Birmingham, Ala., is generally regarded as Maury County's first full-fledged dairy. Involved as he was in the business and social life of his time, it is a tribute to this remarkable man that he still found time to serve the First Methodist Church of Columbia as a member of its Board of Stewards for more than half a century.

Among the special blessings Mr. Williams counted on earth was seeing his eldest daughter, Margaret, a beautiful and brilliant young musician, go forth from the KENNEDY PLACE to become the bride of Sir Asger Hamerik, the celebrated Dane who once headed the Peabody Conservatory of Music in Baltimore.

SKIPWITH HALL
Circa 1818
A first piano and the family coffins

Lean, lanky James Monroe was still in the White House, and Maury County had barely climbed from the cradle of its founding when the colorful biography of SKIPWITH HALL had its first beginnings. Far and away the most outstanding antebellum landmark on the Columbia-Williamsport Pike, SKIPWITH HALL has been with us for more than 150 years.

Its foundations sunk hip-deep and strong in a parcel of Gen. Nathanael Greene's 25,000 acre Revolutionary land grant, this fine old place was built around 1818 by the General's son-in-law, Edward Brinley Littlefield—erstwhile Rhode Islander—second husband of his first cousin and a man who believed in preparing for the hand-hewn uncertainty of life in early Middle Tennessee.

For a sprawling 1100 acre estate to be named LITTLEFIELD may have seemed somewhat ludicrous. That it was christened to honor the memory of Cornelia Littlefield's first husband, Peyton Skipwith, was unique, to say the least. No less unusual, however, were certain of SKIPWITH HALL'S original furnishings. Among the real conversation pieces were Maury County's first piano and a personal coffin for each member of the Littlefield household. An instant delight of friends and neighbors, Cornelia's piano took for itself an immediate place of honor in the family parlor, while the much whispered-about Coffin Room near the head of the stair would be left to weave about SKIPWITH HALL a legend that has lingered here until this very day.

The 1830's were hard-fisted years for this great old house. What the mighty cyclone of '33 ripped and tore at but left behind, the financial Panic of '37 swept away. Edward Littlefield, never a gambler himself, had endorsed one too many notes with one too many of his speculating friends.

If misplaced faith and bursting bubbles had been Edward Littlefield's downfall, SKIPWITH HALL was destined for a new mantle of prosperity at the hand of its next lord and master, colorful Maj. Ben F. Harlan of Kentucky. Under the Major, the addition of six white pillars and a grand veranda became the immediate order of the day. Thanks to the skill and dedication to detail of Maury County's master builder, Nathan Vaught, SKIPWITH HALL'S humble frontier demeanor was transformed into a classic monument to the Planter Age of Middle Tennessee.

During Maj. Harlan's lifetime his home had its own special trademark of hospitality. A little Negro slave boy, stationed in the shade of a mighty oak along the pike, stood ever ready with a cool drink of spring water for each and every passerby in what is now the long gone world of SKIPWITH HALL.

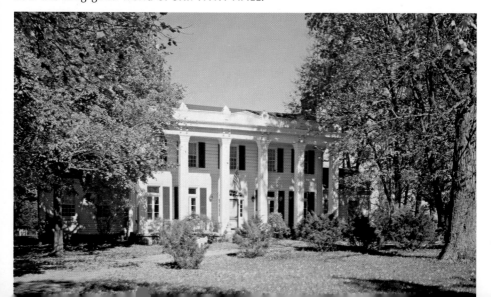

ARKLAND

1848

A generous heart and healthy hogs

But for a lady of gentle birth and tender leanings, there would have been no ARK-LAND.

When wealthy Dr. Gerrard Truman Greenfield died in 1847, his beautiful second wife, Maryland-born Jane Hawkins Dorsett, was left childless and nineteen years her husband's junior. If this ever placed a particular void in her life, there was certainly no lacking in the generosity of this young widow's heart. To Dr. Greenfield's children by his first wife, she graciously gave their original Maury County home and built ARKLAND the next year.

Wealthy in her own right as a daughter of old Col. Fielder Dorsett, an early day shipping tycoon of Anne Arundel County, Md., Jane Greenfield had been left even more so by her late husband. To insure a future heir to her own estate, she had prevailed on a nephew, Thomas Jefferson Dorsett, to forsake his native state and move with his family to Maury County.

Another Dorsett, Thomas Jefferson's nephew, Marion, a frequent visitor to ARKLAND in early life, would gain worldwide fame in agricultural circles as the discoverer of a serum to prevent Hog Cholera in farm livestock.

FAIRMONT
1837
Five hearses brought them home

If regal old FAIRMONT today hails the glories of an age long past, it has also been a temple of bitter tears.

Begun around 1831, FAIRMONT was some six years in the building. Conceived by John Smiser as the twelve-roomed crown jewel of his life; death, sometime in 1840, would make FAIRMONT also his final legacy.

A Marylander by birth, youth had taken John Smiser first to Paris, Ky., for a bride and thence downriver to the bluffs of Natchez and a profitable career as a young attorney of the territorial Bar. Though none can say just when lawyer Smiser began to dream dreams of the Middle Tennessee heartlands, 1816 found the Smisers setting up housekeeping in a two story cedar lodge near the Columbia end of the Old Mooresville Pike. Nearby, some fifteen years later, John Smiser would sink the foundations of his beloved FAIRMONT.

A child of his age, John Smiser thought with the mind of his time. If FAIRMONT'S doors must swing on English hinges and be unlocked by British brass, his own slaves and the good earth of his Mooresville Pike plantation would furnish the timber, clay and stone to be mortised, baked and chiseled into FAIRMONT'S final splendor. Not satisfied with anything but the best of everything, John Smiser's largest single outlay, $9,999 paid to a crew of outside skilled artisans, was considered extremely extravagant for that day and time.

For John Smiser, however, his castle seems to have strangely been built on the shifting sands of joy and sorrow. His death shortly after FAIRMONT'S completion was followed all too soon by that of his widow. Title to the Mooresville Pike properties now fell to daughter Ellen and her husband, James Gray Booker. The new mistress and master of FAIRMONT had no way of knowing then that more tears must soon be shed on the shore of the near future.

If, for a time at least, FAIRMONT'S third floor grand ballroom would ring with lilting waltzes and gay soirees of Old South abundance, a summer's day in 1853 would bring the sad news from New Orleans that four Booker nieces and a brother-in-law had all died of Yellow Fever within a single two-week span.

That following spring, after the quarantine had been lifted, the long shadow of FAIRMONT would fall mournfully across five black hearses, creaking their way slowly over its spacious lawns toward the family burial plot and John Smiser's final resting place.

The famous stone fences of Middle Tennessee have stood for generations. So carefully were they fitted together that mortar was not necessary to guarantee their endurance against the elements.

ELM SPRINGS

1837

A gift from a loving brother

But for a faithful servant, elegant old ELM SPRINGS may have been swept into the ashes of the past by a burning broom.

If the proof is in the pudding, there can be little doubt that James Dick put his only sister, Sarah, on the pedestal of his bachelorhood when he built ELM SPRINGS as a gift to her in 1837.

A lucrative brokerage business with two brothers in New Orleans had enabled James Dick to travel earlier in Europe and acquire a distinct taste for the finer things in life. Some say that when he built ELM SPRINGS he embodied many features of a particular Italian villa that had intrigued his sensitive eye. One marked innovation for that day and time was the placement of a two story ell at one end of the main house rather than in the traditional rear. Instead of a separate smokehouse, meat was hung in a room on the upstairs floor of this ell to be simultaneously cured by the daily rising smoke from the kitchen directly below. Toward the tail end of the Civil War the family chickens were hidden away in this second story smokehouse, only to have the crowing of a loud-mouthed rooster betray their hiding place to a hungry detachment of Yankee foragers.

Obviously enthralled with the pure classicism of ancient Greece and Rome, James Dick had four handsomely conceived Doric columns strung across the front of sister Sarah's fine new Maury County home. Not content with elegant pretense alone and never one to settle for half measures, he saw to it that all fourteen of ELM SPRING'S spacious rooms were lavishly furnished with the finest imported pieces a healthy and generous purse could buy.

Proof that a number of Civil War skirmishes took place uncomfortably close to this old house is furnished by a number of bullet holes still to be found in its great white front pillars. During these turbulently trying times, the family's 18th century silver service was discretely deposited in the secret sanctity of a nearby old cistern and spared the 'five-finger discount' of some erstwhile Yankee marauder.

That ELM SPRINGS still stands resplendent in the sunlight of our own present time is not without a footprint of irony from that distant day when a burning broom, set afire and hidden in a closet by an unknown Yankee soldier, was discovered and hastily extinguished by an unknown family slave.

BOOKER PLACE
1828
Love's labor not lost here

The BOOKER PLACE near Culleoka is living proof that ardent love and patient toil can work together to produce a miracle.

Built in 1828 by Merritt H. Booker, a transplanted Virginian, this genuine gem of a house represents one of Middle Tennessee's most courageous modern-day restorations.

Merritt Booker had ventured down into these parts sometime in the 1820's to join his brother, Peter, soon destined to be known as the richest man in Maury County. Between them, these two Booker brothers soon established strong family ties with another important clan of their day—the Smisers of FAIRMONT. Through marriage, one of Peter's sons would become the second lord and master of the Smisers' extensive Old Mooresville Pike properties. Another inter-family merger would eventually bring the BOOKER PLACE under the hand of one of the Smiser sons.

Sometime in the 1880's title to the Bookers' Culleoka homeplace passed to one Jonas Ingram, grandfather of the man who would rescue this fine old house from the ashes of the past.

Debauched by the whims of neglect and maligned by the weight of too many years, the BOOKER PLACE must have seemed like an impossible task when its present owner, Dan Ingram, began his labor of love in the mid-1960's. Today, from its quaintly charming cellar Keeping Room to its multi-dormered roof, this modest Middle Tennessee gentleman, with his keen eye for detail and a few strokes of luck along the way, has performed a restoration miracle.

In putting together the pieces of the past puzzle of the BOOKER PLACE, Dan Ingram made two important discoveries—a portion of one of the original columns and an old chest of carpenter's tools containing a number of shaper bits that matched the existing interior moldings. The portion of column, plus discolorations on the brick of the front wall, provided this meticulous craftsman with the shape and proportions of the original entrance portico. A sharpening of the old bits enabled him to run off each of the interior moldings that had to be replaced.

Lovers of the fine houses of early Middle Tennessee must always be indebted to Dan Ingram, a humble and ingenious man who accepted an impossible task and made it possible.

The Keeping Room is a part of the devoted restoration of Culleoka's BOOKER PLACE.

MARYMONT
1832
Nine bear dogs and a blazing fire

The roots of MARYMONT reach back into the earliest vitals of Middle Tennessee history. Sedately proud beneath the glorious splendor of its autumn maples, this fine old place was built by Morgan Fitzpatrick in 1832.

Just twenty-six years earlier, nudged by the typical restlessness of his Irish origins and following the keen instincts of the frontier hunter, Morgan Fitzpatrick had ventured into the lower reaches of Maury County around 1806. His proudest possessions had been a brand-new Williamson County bride and nine yowling bear dogs. The young couple's first winter would be spent huddled together in a three-sided shelter of oiled tarpaulins, pitched before a blazing fire in a rough-hewn world of ornery wolves and hostile Indians.

Rubbing shoulders with the hazards of these early days often called for more courage than good sense. Once, when one of Morgan Fitzpatrick's best bear dogs had wandered into a nearby Indian camp, this hard-headed Irishman had calmly strode into camp, called his dog and just as calmly walked away.

With this same quiet resolution, Morgan Fitzpatrick would parlay a three-cornered shelter and nine bear dogs into a considerable fortune. By 1818 he had raised the walls of his first Maury County home near what is today the little farming hamlet of Culleoka. Fourteen years later, his purse fatted by the fertile fields of these Middle Tennessee hinterlands, Morgan Fitzpatrick would build MARYMONT to look down on the 'Sleepy Hollow' world of present day Mooresville.

At his death in 1860 this remarkable man, wielding the axe of raw courage and hard work, had chopped out for himself a 3,000 acre land domain and an estate worth more than $325,000.

A legislative edict of 1836 brought the site of MARYMONT inside the newly formed boundaries of Marshall County. Small wonder today that two illustrious Middle Tennessee counties point a special finger of pride at the regal old house six generations of Fitzpatricks have always called, "Home."

ANTRIM

Circa 1810-1840
From a tiny acorn

Two-storied and humble enough in its beginnings, the oldest portion of ANTRIM claims a special distinction. It can remember what it was like to be Maury County's first brick house south of Duck River.

Stacked one room atop another, with a ground level entrance hall, the ANTRIM Joseph Brown Porter built here around 1810 cast but a meager shadow of the AN-TRIM it would one day become.

Though it fell far below the mark of pretension, Joseph Porter's early Middle Tennessee homestead had what it took to shirk off the long reaching rigors of the great New Madrid Earthquake of 1811. If its terrifying tremors had been enough to carve out famous Reelfoot Lake in the northwestern part of the state, they could manage no more than a simple crack in the eighteen-inch brick walls of ANTRIM. This crack is still pointed to today with a singular kind of pride as proof-positive of this old place's early building date.

Joseph Porter and his first cousin, Col. Joseph Brown, had ventured into the Duck River country around 1806. Both were definitely on hand here when the first court met at Col. Brown's Dec. 21 of the following year and elected Joseph Porter as its clerk. At this time the Porter family was living in a temporary log cabin near the present site of ANTRIM, some four miles south of Columbia and just east of the Pulaski Pike.

Sometime in the 1840's ANTRIM enjoyed a white-pillared face-lifting from its new owner, John Morning Francis. The size of Joseph Porter's original house was more than doubled in this latter day remodeling. With a final flourish of elegant simplicity the demure and humble demeanor of this frontier Middle Tennessee offspring had been helped across the threshold of its crude beginnings and ushered into the more elaborate Planter Age of the Old South. From a tiny acorn, a fine oak had grown.

BEECHLAWN
Circa 1860
". . . the walls of Jericho . . ."

If BEECHLAWN can never forget the muffled roll of distant drums, it may well be because history has often marched across the threshold of this old place.

Aside from its rightful claim as one of Maury County's finest and best preserved Greek Revival homes, BEECHLAWN has a unique distinction all its own. Three of the Civil War's most famous generals used this house as a headquarters during the eventful winter months of November and December, 1864.

When Amos and Cornelia Warfield began BEECHLAWN shortly after their marriage in 1853, the gathering storm that would one day blow their way seemed far removed from the Camelot life of Middle Tennessee's landed gentry. These were those ethereal times when a man's first concern was how many bales of cotton to the acre and his lady could pick and choose from the finest of everything his wealth could buy.

During the seven years it took to build BEECHLAWN, the Warfields made their home in the little log cabin that still stands today at the rear of this old place.

If the guns of Fort Sumter would send Amos Warfield off to fight for the Confederacy in the spring of '61, three years later the Civil War would come surging up Pulaski Pike toward BEECHLAWN.

November, 1864, found Union Gen. John Schofield in full retreat toward Nashville. For a time, when it looked like the thing to do was to turn and fight the Rebels just south of Columbia, BEECHLAWN became Schofield's temporary headquarters. Once, however, he decided to move his troops to safety across Duck River, his bed at BEECHLAWN would hardly have a chance to cool when up rode Gen. Hood. Looking like a one-legged, long-bearded Old Testament prophet, John Bell Hood of Texas had come here with fire in his eye to see the walls of Jericho come tumbling down.

During Hood's brief stay at BEECHLAWN, Mrs. Warfield's library was the scene of a bitter argument between the commanding general and Nathan Bedford Forrest, two of the hottest heads and sharpest tongues in the whole Confederate army. The source of the trouble was a difference of opinion on how best to deal with Schofield's Yankees—a subject that would be a bone of contention more than once during the next few disastrous days.

Within a matter of weeks, after Hood's shattering defeat at Nashville, Forrest would return to BEECHLAWN. This time he would be here to oversee the final retreat of the Confederate army from Middle Tennessee. The very next day, to make sure Hood stayed gone forever, Union Gen. John Schofield and 40,000 men once again paid their respects at BEECHLAWN. This time they also helped themselves to every ham in every smokehouse, gathered up every chicken and burned every fence rail for miles around. By way of an apology, some months later when Maj. Warfield fell into Federal hands, Gen. Schofield personally intervened and saw to the Major's safe return to BEECHLAWN—a grand old Maury County house that may never cease to listen for the sound of distant drums and the tramp of marching feet on the slopes of the eternal past.

The 'First Family' of BEECHLAWN made their home in this log cabin while their grand Middle Tennessee house was being built.

Through the front entrance of BEECHLAWN strode some of the most famous generals of the Civil War. Both the Union's Gen. John Schofield and the Confederacy's John Bell Hood used this house as a temporary headquarters. BEECHLAWN'S library, just off this entrance hall, was the scene of a famous argument between Hood and Gen. Nathan Bedford Forrest.

WILSON PLACE
1834
Gone but not forgotten

When Nathan Vaught built this fine old place for Robert Wilson in 1834, he made himself $500 for his efforts and gave Maury County a house it has always been proud to claim as its own.

According to his own records, it took from May, 1833, until the following March for builder Vaught to finish this house of eight spacious rooms, divided above and below by two halls of equal proportion. Built entirely of brick burned on the premises, Rob Wilson's new home was floored with white ash and boasted woodwork and moldings of rich native cherry. Its handsomely fanlighted entrance, second to none in Middle Tennessee, would offer the gracious hospitality of this house to some of the most famous names in the Old South's days of plush and plenty.

Mounted atop a five-roomed cellar, with a full attic above, WILSON PLACE soon became known far and wide for its most unusual downstairs mantels. Uniquely stenciled and lacquered in gold, these conversation pieces were always a source of wonder and admiration for all who came to know and love this old house through the passing years.

When Dr. and Mrs. Tom K. Young bought WILSON PLACE in 1957, they furnished their new homeplace on Greene Road with an extraordinary collection of antiques and family portraits. Counted among the many fine pieces the Youngs brought with them were three chairs that once belonged to Robert E. Lee. There were also priceless heirlooms of French silver over two centuries old. To the sorrow of everyone, all of these treasures would be lost when fire swept through WILSON PLACE in the early hours of June 10, 1972—just three weeks to the day after this picture was taken by the author.

The Youngs, away from home at the time of the fire, were later gratified to find that despite the terrific heat the foundation and first floor walls were still sound enough to permit the rebuilding of a one story version of the old house that would always claim a special place in their hearts.

PILLOW PLACE
Circa 1845
Fried ham and murdered sons

No two families in Middle Tennessee built finer Greek Revival houses than the Polks and Pillows of Maury County.

If the first Gideon Pillow in these parts was a rough-and-tumble ex-Indianfighter and early land surveyor, he would rear three polished gentlemen for sons. Each would be endowed with an appetite to live life in the grand manner of his day, and each would hold sufficient purse strings to settle for nothing less.

Had old Gideon Pillow lived long enough, he would have been proud that his second son, Granville, chose to build his house on the very same site of the family's first hearthstone in Maury County.

Granville Pillow's house, featuring four Ionic columns that reach to monumental heights above Campbellsville Pike, was originally christened ROSE HILL but has come to be known in our own time simply as the PILLOW PLACE.

As the second jewel in the grand tiara of Pillow homes in Maury County, this old house, completed sometime around 1845, has been hailed by architects as one of the finest examples of neo-classic architecture in all of Middle Tennessee. It has also played host to one of the Civil War's most fascinating characters.

Still smarting from the licking the Army had taken three days before at the Battle of Nashville, Gen. Nathan Bedford Forrest was entertained here on the night of Dec. 19, 1864, by Maj. Granville Pillow. A young Rebel staff officer, Capt. James Dinkins, recalled years later how everyone's morale seemed to get a sudden boost the next morning from ". . . a big dish of fried ham and plenty of bread and coffee . . ."

When the bitter pills of defeat and despair were handed out, PILLOW PLACE would have its turn to swallow. As if things were not made bad enough by the ordinary trials and tribulations of Reconstruction, news would travel north from Huntsville on Jan. 9, 1870, that two young Pillow sons—Granville, Jr., and his brother, William—had been mysteriously murdered and robbed near the little farming hamlet of Leighton, Ala.

If the brothers' childhood home had first been named ROSE HILL, it is with a touch of irony that both should sleep their final sleep side by side in Columbia's Rose Hill Cemetery.

POLK HOME
1816
His word—his bond

After a long, hard look at the past, history has decided that James Knox Polk was one of this nation's truly great Presidents.

Small wonder that two states like to claim this most remarkable man. If Knox Polk was born in Mecklenburg County, N.C., Nov. 2, 1795, he was only a boy of eleven when he moved with his family to Middle Tennessee. As the first of ten children of Samuel and Jane Knox Polk, young manhood briefly carried him back to his native Tarheel State to graduate Salutatorian of the University of North Carolina's Class of 1818. It was, however, as a Tennessean that James Knox Polk would make his marks on the scrolls of history.

He would begin to sharpen his pen the very next year as a young clerk in the Nashville law offices of His Honor, Judge Felix Grundy—future U.S. Senator from Tennessee and one day Attorney General to President Martin Van Buren.

Once back home in Columbia, Knox Polk, always more of a believer in perspiration than inspiration, was the kind of hard-working young attorney of the Bar who could not go unnoticed. When it came time for Maury County to fill a seat in the State

The President's personal trunk, pistols and miniature.

James K. Polk has come to be reflected in the true light of history as one of this country's truly great Presidents. During this hard-working man's four years in the White House, he left Washington City only once.

Legislature in 1823, twenty-eight-year-old James Knox Polk was the man the voters sent to Murfreesboro. This began the rise of the Polk political sun that would not set before it had shone for four fruitful years on the White House.

James Knox Polk was still a freshman legislator when the folks in his home District sent him to Congress in 1825. As a political protégé and House floor leader for his good friend, President Andrew Jackson, when Old Hickory had a Congressional job to be done he looked to young Knox Polk to do it.

Still in Congress in 1839, Polk's last two terms were as Speaker of the House, a feat claimed by no other President before or since. When the Democrats found themselves in trouble that year in the race for Tennessee's Governorship, this humble and self-effacing man would sacrifice his career on the altar of his Party's good. Told by local political leaders and old Andy Jackson himself, "If anyone can beat them, you can," Polk turned his back on the House Speakership, made the 1839 governor's race and won.

If becoming Governor of Tennessee would have brought political midnight to most, it was not to be so for Knox Polk. Considered this nation's first "dark horse" candidate for the Presidency in 1844, he won that, too. While his Whig opponents were still scratching their heads and wondering, "Who is James K. Polk?", at forty-nine, he had been elected his country's youngest President up to that time.

From the outset, Polk had sworn to never seek a second term. When all of the chips of his accomplishments were counted, he did not need one. James Knox Polk of Tennessee was the only President in our history to work at his job long and hard enough to nail every single plank of his Party's platform into place in the short span of a single term. Only once during the whole four years, did he leave Washington—for a brief, get-acquainted trip to New England. This would be the only time folks outside the capital city would get a good look at this gray-eyed miracle worker from Tennessee. Before Knox Polk's day in court was done, he would add Texas to the Union—settle the Oregon question with England—wrench California from the Mexicans—gain us equal rights on the High Seas—revise the protective tariff and put it to work paying some of the fare of government—consecrate the Naval Academy at Annapolis—and die within three months after leaving office—literally worked to death. James Knox Polk has proved he was the kind of man who never quit plowing until he reached the last fence row.

To the sadness of a grateful nation, he died at his Nashville home, POLK PLACE, at the early age of fifty-four.

If POLK PLACE, like its distinguished master, is gone now, his ancestral home in Columbia has been a shrine to the memory of our eleventh President since its opening to the public in early 1930.

Visited by thousands annually, Columbia's POLK HOME is where young James Knox Polk turned the corner of his twenty-first year and his footsteps toward the future.

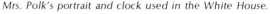

Mrs. Polk's portrait and clock used in the White House.

43

Official White House china.

Known to history as "Young Hickory," Pres. Polk was especially proud of this bust of Andrew Jackson.

Built in 1816 by the President's father, Samuel Polk, this is the house once presided over by the first woman in Knox Polk's life, his mother—Jane Knox Polk. This devout Presbyterian lady would live long enough to see her son in the highest office in the land and to comfort him on the deathbed of his final illness.

The POLK HOME in Columbia is also where Knox Polk presented to his family and friends the only other woman in his life, his blushingly beautiful bride of 1824—the former Sarah Childress of Murfreesboro. Perhaps the best description of Sarah Childress Polk came from the British Ambassador while her husband was in the White House. "Madam," he said, "there is a woe pronounced against you in the Bible." When Mrs. Polk was puzzled, the Ambassador explained, "The Bible says woe unto you when all men speak well of you."

Since the ancestral POLK HOME and that of the President's two sisters next door, are the only two houses left anywhere to enshrine the life and memory of James Knox Polk—a truly great American—any trip to Middle Tennessee without a visit here would be like a trek through Egypt without seeing the pyramids.

Side view of the POLK HOME showing the residence of his sisters.

Parlor of the POLK HOME. Table in the foreground was a gift of the Presidential years.

ST. PETER'S EPISCOPAL CHURCH
After 1860
Great bishops and dead generals

ST. PETER'S EPISCOPAL CHURCH in Columbia will always have a very special place in the lore and legend of Middle Tennessee. Since the founding of its congregation in 1828, its pulpit has furnished four outstanding southern bishops: James H. Otey and W. Fred Gates, Jr. of Tennessee; Leonidas Polk of Louisiana; and Thomas N. Carruthers, Bishop of South Carolina.

With much ado on a Wednesday afternoon, Sept. 5, 1860, the cornerstone of ST. PETER'S EPISCOPAL CHURCH was laid by the Rev. David Pise, with future Bishop of Tennessee, Charles T. Quintard, standing-in for an ailing Bishop Otey.

ST. PETER'S was still unfinished when the Federals commandeered the building and grounds as their provost marshal headquarters in March of '62. Since Columbia was dubbed by the Yankees as "Camp Morehead" and turned into a military garrison, anyone entering or leaving town had to stop by ST. PETER'S for a pass signed by Union Col. Jeremiah Green. Legend says this historic old church also doubled as a barracks and hospital during the occupation and credits John Baird, a junior warden, with preventing the sanctuary from being burned to the ground on one occasion.

Later in the War the funerals of four Confederate generals would be preached from the pulpit of ST. PETER'S. The first was that of Gen. Earl Van Dorn, slain at his headquarters desk in nearby Spring Hill on May 7, 1863. Eighteen months later last rights would be said here for Pat Cleburne, O. F. Strahl and H. B. Granbury, three of five Rebel generals to die at the Battle of Franklin.

For generations now ST. PETER'S handsomely turreted bell tower, completed in 1871, has been calling Columbians to worship each and every Sunday in one of the most beautiful church sanctuaries in all of Middle Tennessee.

The sanctuary of ST. PETER'S EPISCOPAL CHURCH is one of the most inspiringly beautiful in all of Middle Tennessee. Here were held the funeral services of Confederate Generals Van Dorn, Cleburne, Strahl and Granbury during the Civil War. A memorial window to Gen. and Mrs. R. S. Ewell is particularly interesting.

45

RALLY HILL
Circa 1843
They drew the line here.

Situated on the site of a once gushing and locally famous old spring, RALLY HILL was built around 1843 by James Walker, a brother-in-law of the eleventh President of the United States.

Long before James Knox Polk climbed out of the shadows of obscurity and into the presidential chair, James Walker had been making his own waves in the life and times of early Maury County. Not only was he the publisher of Columbia's first newspaper, The Western Chronicle, but a pioneer in a huge iron industry that once flourished in these parts. The cast gutters that even today still gird the eaves of RALLY HILL are lasting mementos of James Walker's ventures in Maury County's early iron industry.

As the home of Jane Marie Polk Walker, the sister of the President, RALLY HILL was also the ancestral hearthstone of three outstanding sons. Each, in his own way, would leave a special mark on the page of Columbia's early history.

On a four acre gift of land from his father, Samuel Polk Walker contracted with Nathan Vaught, in 1835, to build a most unique Gothic house that has come to be known far and wide as the ATHENAEUM RECTORY.

A second son of the Walkers, Joseph Knox, served as private secretary to his President-uncle during the Polk years in the White House. As a colonel in the Confederacy, Joseph would die at the highwater mark of the War in 1863.

A third Walker boy, Lucius Marshall, had graduated from West Point in 1850, risen to the rank of brigadier general in the Confederate Army, only to die of a wound from a duel with another southern general, John S. Marmaduke.

At James Walker's death a most unusual method was used to settle his estate. A chalk line was drawn through the stair hall of RALLY HILL so that a completely equitable division of the old homeplace could be made among his heirs.

ATHENAEUM RECTORY

1835-1837

A Confederate from Vermont

With its notched battlements and triple-arched entrance, Columbia's ATHENAEUM RECTORY may well have belonged to the Middle Ages.

Restored to perfection and open to the public today, this old place is a lasting reminder that Columbia was once the home of two of the South's most outstanding finishing schools for young ladies.

Begun in 1835 by master artisan Nathan Vaught as a residence for Samuel Polk Walker, a nephew of President Polk, this house was completed two years later as the home of the Rev. F. G. Smith, the new rector of Columbia Female Institute.

A native of Vermont, Franklin Gillette Smith had given up a church and school in Lynchburg, Va., to come to Columbia at the invitation of Leonidas Polk and James H. Otey, two of the founders of the Institute.

In 1852 Rev. Smith resigned his position at Columbia Female Institute to found his own school. His home now became the Rectory of the Columbia Athenaeum, an elegant and fashionable finishing school for girls. In its heyday this institution boarded as many as 125 young ladies from both sides of the Mason-Dixon Line.

Although the old Rectory is all that is left of Rev. Smith's school, the Athenaeum originally had a sprawling, tree-shaded campus that boasted a number of handsome buildings in the classic style of Old South splendor.

By the outbreak of the Civil War, the Rev. Smith had become a "converted Yankee." He left little doubt where his sympathies lay when, from his own pocket, he equipped a whole company of troops—the Maury Rifles—for service in the Confederate Army. He would pay for such loyalty to his adopted homeland when the Federals invaded Columbia early in the War and commandeered his residence as a military headquarters.

With almost three years of sporadic fighting in this region of Middle Tennessee, when friend and foe alike took turns occupying the town, gallant officers of both sides danced more than one gay soiree in the gala halls of the old ATHENAEUM RECTORY. One of the most lavish of all the balls staged here during those colorful days was one honoring Gen. Nathan Bedford Forrest, the Confederacy's 'wizard of the saddle' and a native son of Tennessee.

When Rev. Smith died in 1866, he was so esteemed and beloved his is said to have been the largest funeral ever held in Columbia.

The Athenaeum continued operations for another thirty-seven years after its distinguished founder's death. In 1903 its buildings and grounds were sold to the City and used as a public high school until around 1915 when these old landmarks were demolished in favor of a more modern educational complex.

The old Rectory remained in the Smith family until 1974 when it was given to the Association for the Preservation of Tennessee Antiquities.

MERCER HALL
1838
Fifty-seven broken windowpanes and two men of God

By 1872 MERCER HALL had fallen from its original grace. Raised into bloom by the tender touch of a man of God, this fine old house, thirty-four years later, stood forlorn and empty—raped by the wrath of war and debased by the waif of neglect.

MERCER HALL was built in 1838 by Episcopal clergyman William Leacock, server of his Master's flock not only in Columbia but also at old St. Mark's Church in Williamsport. In time, however, an even more imposing shadow of The Cloth would fall across the lawns of MERCER HALL with the coming of the Rt. Rev. James H. Otey—first Episcopal Bishop of Tennessee, founder of the Columbia Institute for Young Women, guiding light and first chancellor of the University of the South at Sewanee.

Built on a plot of ground that was once President James K. Polk's vegetable garden, MERCER HALL, following Bishop Otey's tenure, was destined to know the humiliation of horses stabled in its basement during the Civil War and boarders being fed in its grand banquet hall in the lean wake of its aftermath.

If the sister of Confederate General Gideon Pillow, Narcissa Martin, was determined to save the homeplace she had bought from Bishop Otey, this lady of gentle birth was no match for the much harder times of a South prostrate in defeat. Just as her

Rear parlor in MERCER HALL.

eager patrons devoured the fruits of her table, so did the destitution of Reconstruction gobble up her valiant efforts to save her beloved MERCER HALL.

By January, 1872, the magnificent heritage of this fine old house hung in tatters, and MERCER HALL was left to stand alone against the winter world of Middle Tennessee. Creaking on the joints of decayed sills, tugged at from within by the eerie squeak of many an unlatched door, this courageous old place—staring through the shattered dreams of fifty-seven broken windowpanes—never seemed to give up hope that somewhere, out of this despondency and its devout beginnings, would spring the glorious resurrection it knows today.

The gazebo in the rear garden of MERCER HALL once graced the campus of one of the Old South's most famous finishing schools for young ladies.

BLYTHEWOOD
Circa 1859
A poet in soldier's clothing

Almost completely hidden from the rest of the world by eight sprawling acres of wooded wonderland, BLYTHEWOOD brings to the Cumberland foothills of Maury County a special French Colonial flavor all its own.

Though the actual construction date of BLYTHEWOOD is as vague as the present remains of its once proud gardens, the laurels for adding this quaintly charming house to the varied portfolio of Middle Tennessee architecture must go to a Virginian.

While still shy of his twentieth year, Thomas Keesee had ventured down from Richmond to Columbia around 1837 and set up shop in line with his trade of carriage maker. That prosperity must have eventually knocked at the door of hard work and frugality is proven by the fact that sometime on the eve of the Civil War coach maker Keesee was able to build a house like BLYTHEWOOD.

Thomas Keesee's tenure as first master of BLYTHEWOOD was, however, of short duration. On the morning of November 27, 1864, a new owner—war-widowed Leonora Wilson—and her daughter, Eugenia, stood on its doorstep. In handkerchief fluttering breathlessness, they watched as Stewart's Corps of the Confederate Army of Tennessee swung past along Mt. Pleasant Pike. Suddenly, to the joy of mother and daughter alike, a thoroughly frayed and tattered young Alabama soldier appeared at BLYTHEWOOD'S front gate—the saga of too many miles beneath his almost shoeless feet, the tale of too few hot breakfasts scrawled across the pinched span of his youthful brow.

That night, in the dim light of a wavering campfire on the outskirts of Columbia, a grateful and thoroughly well-fed Pvt. Junius Jordan, Jr. hunched over his tablet and began to write:

> "Eugenia! Thou beautiful Tennessee sprite!
> Unto thee a few lines, I now will indite.
> Give ear to these words, don't bear them alone;
> Expressed by a soldier lad far from his home.
> Now I give many thanks for your goodness to me
> In my ragged condition in old Tennessee . . ."

Just as the name of its builder, Thomas Keesee, would hang but briefly above BLYTHE-WOOD'S latchstring, so would the kindly Mrs. Wilson and her daughter, Eugenia, soon, also, pass from its stage.

After the Wilsons, there came to BLYTHEWOOD Col. P. C. Bethell of Memphis. From August 30, 1879, to the spring of 1886, Col. Bethell used this house as a summer home, and it was during this time that he gave downtown Columbia one of its best known landmarks—the old Bethell Hotel.

From Col. Bethell the title to BLYTHEWOOD passed to another hotel man, Col. R. E. Rivers, founder and guiding spirit of the famous St. Charles in New Orleans. Col. Rivers, also planning BLYTHEWOOD as a summer retreat, was to have the shortest tenure of all in this fine old house. Two brief months and a soaring thermometer was all it took to convince the good Colonel that he could bake almost as done in Middle Tennessee as in his native Louisiana. Having reached this sweltering conclusion, Col. Rivers sold BLYTHEWOOD to Mr. and Mrs. E. H. Hatcher on a hot August day in 1886.

Unlike any of BLYTHEWOOD'S former owners, the Hatchers would live out the balance of their days in the comfort and wooded beauty of this grand old place.

HUGHES HOUSE
1854
Among Maury's finest

Columbia's stately, handsome HUGHES HOUSE was built by a most distinguished early Middle Tennessee jurist with a most imposing name—Judge Archelaus M. Hughes.

Old records have His Honor purchasing his fourteen-acre homesite from the estate of Patrick McGuire on June 3, 1851. The late Mr. McGuire had earlier made a "princely fortune" in Maury County real estate.

Three years in the building and even today still blessed with spacious surroundings of informal natural beauty, the HUGHES HOUSE, without frill or fanfare, has a subtle and simple dignity that will always rank it high on the lengthy list of Maury County's finer antebellum homes.

PARSONS PLACE
1858
In the shape of a cross

Raised in part out of logs from the original Zion Presbyterian Church, Columbia's PARSONS PLACE dates back to 1858.

This unique little Gothic gem, laid out in the shape of a cross, was built by the man who set the cornerstone of St. Peter's Episcopal Church, the Rev. David Pise.

Built more than 100 years ago by a man of The Cloth, it is an interesting coincidence that this fine old place today finds itself owned by a family of Parsons.

STRATTON-DOUGLAS HOUSE
1850's
In a world of its own

If not a great deal is known about its early history, the STRATTON-DOUGLAS HOUSE in Columbia adds the distinct flavor of dignified simplicity to the varied architectural punchbowl of antebellum Middle Tennessee.

Built by J. H. Stratton sometime in the 1850's and once known as THE PINES, this humble treasure of a house lies half hidden from the rest of the world, tucked quietly away in its own special fairyland of flowering dogwoods and redbud.

LOONEY HOUSE
Circa 1835
Host to an unwelcome guest

As Columbia's LOONEY HOUSE looks back over the shoulder of the past, it can remember a Yankee trooper galloping through its hallway and has the scars to prove it.

With a flair for Gothic columns and a handsomely transomed entrance, this fine old Federal townhouse has seen more than its share of the joys and sorrows of life in early Middle Tennessee.

Though the whims of future owners would furnish additions and alterations, the earliest portion of this old place was built by David Looney, a rising young attorney, about the time of his marriage in 1835 to Miss Mary Ann McGuire.

Although her sister, Ellen, would reign for more than a half century as the grande dame of the MAYES-FRIERSON PLACE, just a block up the street, Mary Ann Looney was not meant long to walk this earth. As early as 1839, in deep despair over his young wife's untimely death, David Looney sold their home to Pleasant Nelson, another prominent Columbian. This same year saw Mr. Nelson engage master builder Nathan Vaught to erect a four-room brick addition, accompanied by a rather spacious veranda looking east toward Garden St.

In 1854 the LOONEY HOUSE had taken on still another owner, the W. S. Fleming family. However, by the time the first Federals came to these heights above Duck River, the Flemings had forsaken their townhouse and moved into a newer home on the outskirts of Columbia. The LOONEY HOUSE, once found to be unoccupied, was immediately taken over by the Union invaders as an officers' quarters. Traces of blood-stains found in more recent times indicate that this old place may also have seen service as a Yankee hospital during the many skirmishes in and around Columbia.

Still another memento of these turbulent times is a long, ugly scar on the ashen floor of the LOONEY HOUSE'S entrance hall. Lingering legend insists it was gouged out by a riotous "Blue Belly" who rode his horse up the front steps and into the house during the Occupation.

Insult was added to injury when the Flemings' country home suddenly burned to the ground in the throes of these bitter days and left them no choice but to return to town and throw themselves on the mercy of the Federal authorities. Since Union officers were still cooling their heels in the LOONEY HOUSE, the Flemings were granted permission to tack onto its west side a humble three-room addition in which to sit and listen for the final echo of rattling sabres, distant drums and marching men.

MAYES PLACE
1854
Toward the river—an underground exit

Once Samuel Mayes decided to build himself a fine town house in the heart of Columbia, he obviously turned loose the purse strings of a rather handsome fortune.

If the MAYES PLACE'S massive Corinthian columns were to reach higher than most, perfectly patterned formal gardens—in all of their Victorian splendor—would soon wander across their long falling shadows. Almost five acres in all, Samuel Mayes' gardens were destined to become the pride of antebellum Columbia and the envy of Middle Tennessee's "golden gentry" of that day.

Samuel Mayes' house, however, reaches back much further than Victorian England for the source of its inspiration, farther back even than the great Georgian homes of the Virginia Tidewater.

Like so many of his affluent contemporaries, this merchant prince of Middle Tennessee thirsted for the crystal clear classicism of esthetic Greece, yet hungered, too, for the enduring practicality of ancient Rome. He might crown the columns of his house with delicate acanthus leaves, but its balconies must be girded with railings of everlasting iron. If Samuel Mayes fancied a gently pitched pediment, all door and window lintels would be arched with the same stoney strength that had sent long miles of aqueducts sprawling across the world of the Caesars and left a Colosseum to defy the ages.

Today, though the grand gardens of Samuel Mayes' town house have been raked smooth by the prongs of passing years, the legend still persists of a mysterious tunnel running underground all the way to the bluffs of Duck River. Whether such a subterranean exit ever existed, or was no more than a whim of the fanciful mind of the past, no one of our time dares say for sure. That, beneath the eaves and high-browed elegance of the MAYES PLACE, the Leprechauns of grace and beauty seem to be willing to dance forever, few are ready to deny.

54

MAYES-FRIERSON PLACE
1835-1845
The hearthstone of a dynasty

If a harsh word could stir Pat McGuire's Irish temper, the marriage of a favorite daughter could also touch a generous heart.

Ellen McGuire's betrothal to Roger Bradley Mayes in 1833 was the signal for her immigrant Irish father to begin thinking of a befitting wedding present. That same year Patrick McGuire contracted with master craftsman Nathan Vaught to build the house Columbia has known almost forever as the MAYES-FRIERSON PLACE.

Married in 1834, the young newlyweds moved into their new home on W. Sixth St. the very next year. They were just in time for their first child to be born in a house that would remain in the hands of Pat McGuire's descendants for just under the next century and a half.

The new Mrs. Roger Bradley Mayes was one of seven daughters and three sons born to Patrick and Martha McGuire. Perhaps Ellen's marriage had plucked the strings of her father's own romantic memories. It may well have recalled how he had suddenly decided "to settle nearby" after spying a comely sixteen-year-old Irish lass, Martha Kavanaugh, doing the family wash on a Williamson County farm not too many years before.

Just as time has a way of passing, families have a way of growing, and 1845 saw four upstairs bedrooms added to this old house. The earlier sleeping quarters of the west wing became a double parlor, suitable for the lavish entertainment of some of the most notable personages of that day.

For more than a half century of her lifetime, Ellen McGuire Mayes would cherish the wedding gift of a generous father. At her death in 1890, the MAYES-FRIERSON PLACE would be handed down to a granddaughter, then to that granddaughter's daughters until this old house was lived in for 133 years by the offspring of a big-hearted Irishman named Patrick McGuire.

ANNOATUCK
1823
**Beneath a windowsill—
a cannonball**

For more than 150 years the Middle Tennessee wind has brushed the noble brow of ANNOATUCK.

Destined to become Maury County's outstanding architect of antebellum elegance, young Nathan Vaught had barely shed the thongs of his orphaned apprenticeship as a master builder when, sometime in the spring of 1823, he put the finishing touches on this stately old place.

Maj. John Brown II, one of eight sons to share in his father's 5,000 acre Revolutionary land grant, was careful to choose a commanding site for his ". . . two-story brick dwelling house of six rooms and two halls . . . on the north side of Duck River." Appropriately, Maj. Brown christened his new home ANNOATUCK. This poetically descriptive Indian sobriquet, meaning "A Windy Hill," had been bestowed on the Major's lofty perch long before the first white man ever touched his eager toe to the sweet sod of Maury County.

High-ceilinged and wainscoted throughout the first floor, ANNOATUCK is without frill or pretense. Spacious enough without elaboration, each room of ANNOATUCK'S inner sanctum is entered through "Christian doors," crested with the Cross surmounting an open Bible at the bottom. If Nathan Vaught designed these doors to stand vigil against Satan, he may also have meant them as daily reminders of Man's Heavenly needs.

This cannonball slammed into an outside windowsill at ANNOATUCK during the Civil War. Luckily for all concerned, it most graciously failed to explode.

Although Fate did not choose Columbia as one of the Civil War's great battlefields, there was a time when artillery duels back and forth across the Duck River valley got to be almost as common as corn pone and black-eyed peas for the folks at ANNOATUCK. During the skirmishing below Nashville in the latter years of the war, this old place, more often than not, usually found itself within the enemy's lines. The rounded shoulders of Union gun emplacements may still be seen at the rear of the house, but ANNOATUCK'S most cherished memento of those days of sound and fury will always be a Nathan Bedford Forrest cannonball that slammed itself beneath a front windowsill and most graciously failed to explode.

When master artisan Nathan Vaught built a house, he thought of everything, even including built-in closets—an almost unheard-of convenience of his day.

OAKLAWN
1835
If these walls could talk

One of the real question marks of history surrounds handsome old OAKLAWN.

By the afternoon of Nov. 29, 1864, John Bell Hood had managed to get two corps of his Confederate Army of Tennessee between John Schofield and Spring Hill. Only the Union supply train, guarded by a single division, had managed to reach the safety of this little farming hamlet that lay to the north along the Federal line of retreat toward Nashville. The rest of Schofield's army, marching frantically up the Columbia-Franklin Pike, were hopelessly cut off and easily within Hood's grasp.

Convinced that he had made the grandiose flanking move of his career, Hood selected as his temporary headquarters Col. Absalom Thompson's white-pillared house, OAK-LAWN, situated just east of the Pike and about two miles south of Spring Hill. His left arm shattered by a Union ball at Gettysburg, a leg left at Chickamauga and often on laudanum out of almost continuous pain, Gen. Hood, sometime late that afternoon, was unstrapped from his mount and helped into the house that would shroud forever in mystery the events that followed.

Just what happened at OAKLAWN on the night of Nov. 29, 1864, has had scholars of the Civil War scratching their heads for over a century. Did, as some oldtimers assert, Gen. Hood, in foggy-headed revelry, drink up what may well have been the South's last real drop of opportunity? Or, as one of OAKLAWN'S former house servants later philosophized, were the blunders of this night permitted because, "God just didn't want that war to go on no longer."? Whatever the answer, Schofield's escape that night under Hood's very nose would lend a special meaning to Johnny Reb's ensuing quickstep version of The Yellow Rose of Texas:

The entrance hall at OAKLAWN.

> ". . . You may talk about your Beauregard
> And sing of General Lee,
> But the gallant Hood of Texas
> Played hell in Tennessee."

RIPPAVILLA

1850's

Breakfast in the morning—death in the afternoon

No house in history can claim the special kind of fame that belongs to RIPPAVILLA. Of French Huguenot extraction, Nathaniel Cheairs was born in nearby Spring Hill in the Christmas month of 1818. Sometime in the 1850's he had become a young man with means enough to turn his dreams of a house like RIPPAVILLA into a magnificent reality. The site he chose for his Middle Tennessee manor house lay some two miles south of Spring Hill, on the east shoulder of the Columbia-Franklin Pike.

First to be raised were the kitchen and servants' quarters which afforded the Cheairs family a place to live while "the big house" was being built.

When completed RIPPAVILLA was a masterpiece of classic perfection, both inside and out. If other Corinthian columns have reached higher, few have stood prouder or been better proportioned. The attention to exterior detail is superb, while the hospitable balance of the two white-pillared porticoes gives more than a subtle hint of RIPPAVILLA'S lavishly decored interior. Upstairs and down, this house is a treasure. The focal point of the grand entrance hall is a magnificent stairway that needs to play "second fiddle" to none when it comes to delicate grace and sheer elegance. Still another particularly unique feature of RIPPAVILLA'S inner sanctum is its Wedgewood-medallioned mantels, each of which is a breath-taking reminder of that long ago time and place in history when the ultimate in taste and craftsmanship was the rule rather than the exception.

As the husband of the former Susan McKissack of Spring Hill, Nathaniel Cheairs was the brother-in-law of notorious Jessie McKissack Peters, whose romantic entanglements with that Confederate cavalier, Gen. Earl Van Dorn, would lead to dire consequences. On a May day in 1863, Dr. George B. Peters, Jessie's irate husband, would put a pistol ball in Van Dorn's brain as the General sat at his headquarter's desk in nearby FERGUSON HALL, the home of Nathaniel's brother, Martin Cheairs.

Earlier in the War, as a Major of the Third Tennessee Infantry, another dubious distinction had befallen Nathaniel Cheairs. He had been the officer chosen to carry the white flag of surrender to Gen. Grant at the fall of Fort Donelson on the Cumberland River.

RIPPAVILLA'S own special place in history, however, centers around the events of Nov. 30, 1864, when Maj. Cheairs invited Confederate Gen. Hood and his ranking officers of the Army of Tennessee to breakfast at his home before taking out after John Scho-field's Federals who had fled up the Pike the night before.

Seated around the mountain of fried ham, hot biscuits and steaming coffee of RIPPAVILLA'S banquet table that morning were five generals of the Confederacy who would never live to see the sun set on this Indian Summer's day. Pat Cleburne, H. B. Granbury, O. F. Strahl, John Adams and States Rights Gist would all be shot to death this very afternoon in the Battle of Franklin.

FERGUSON HALL
Before 1854
100 years in hiding

Spring Hill's FERGUSON HALL was the scene of one of the most famous murders in Middle Tennessee history. Here, a single pistol shot cost the Confederacy one of its greatest generals.

Long pointed out as the most pretentious white-pillared house in town, FERGUSON HALL was built by Dr. John Haddox, a local physician of much renown.

Sometime shortly before his death in 1854, Dr. Haddox sold his home in Spring Hill to Martin Cheairs. When Martin's brother, Nathaniel, began building RIPPAVILLA just down the Pike toward Columbia, he seems to have kept one eye on FERGUSON HALL for his inspiration. So similar are these houses in proportion and classic detail, no stranger in these parts is ever surprised that they once belonged to two well-to-do brothers.

In the early spring of 1863, Gen. Earl Van Dorn had ridden into Spring Hill as commander of Confederate cavalry in Middle Tennessee. If getting licked by the Yankees at Pea Ridge and Corinth had robbed him of much of his military stature, his reputation as "a ladies' man" would cost him his life. On May 7, Earl Van Dorn was shot to death at his headquarters desk in FERGUSON HALL by a jealous Dr. George B. Peters. The trigger of this tragedy seems to have been cocked by the rumor of a clandestine romance between the General and Jessie Peters, whose empty carriage was seen parked much too often at the rear of FERGUSON HALL.

Although Martin Cheairs died in 1891, his white-pillared house on the hill would stay in the family for another fourteen years. In 1905 Branham and Hughes Academy bought FERGUSON HALL and fifty-seven gently rolling acres for the modern-day amazing sum of $10,000. Chartered originally as Spring Hill Male College, in its heyday this famous Maury County boarding school for boys boasted as many as 300 students from fifteen different states in the Union.

Now a part of the Tennessee Orphans Home, FERGUSON HALL furnished a most unusual discovery in 1963. Exactly 100 years after Gen. Van Dorn was shot to death in this house, Orphanage Director W. R. Richter, searching one day behind a closet wall, fished out a fully-loaded pre-Civil War Colt revolver. This mysterious pistol has lifted many an eyebrow and caused much scratching of heads. Was this the gun George Peters used to kill Earl Van Dorn? If so, why was it still fully-loaded? If not, why was it so carefully hidden so near the scene of the crime that it took a whole century to be found? Perhaps historic old FERGUSON HALL is the only one who will ever be able to answer these intriguing questions.

EWELL FARM
1867
**". . . In their deaths
they were not divided"**

If Richard Stoddert Ewell was a long-beaked, bald-headed ugly duckling in the parlors of his day, he was an eagle on the battlefields of an era. As the hard-hitting "right fist" of the great Stonewall Jackson, EWELL FARM'S most illustrious master had come away from Appomattox the third ranked soldier in Robert E. Lee's immortal Army of Northern Virginia.

The Civil War had found "Dick" Ewell a love-sick, middle-aged bachelor and left him, four years later, the doting, peg-legged bridegroom of his cousin, the widowed Lizenka Campbell Brown—the one woman he had loved for more than half a lifetime. A kneecap shot away at Second Manassas had hurried Lizenka north from Nashville in the summer of '62 to nurse General Ewell back to health and become his bride the following spring.

Named for the Czarina of Russia, where she was born in 1820, the new Mrs. Ewell was the only daughter of her Minister father, Senator George W. Campbell—the man who would one day sell the State of Tennessee the site of its present capitol building. As a woman of high station and strong will, Lizenka Ewell was also the possessor of an imposing dowry that included a handsome tract of land just west of Spring Hill, at the far end of Depot Road. On the crown of a crest, commanding the fertile, gently rolling acres of their new Maury County homeplace, General and "Miss Lizzie" Ewell, in 1867, built the house that would shelter the last five joyous years of their lives together on this earth.

Obviously an offspring of the Victorian Age, EWELL FARM, with its gently bending arches and gracefully arrayed colonettes, adds a distinctly Italianate flavor to the bountiful punch bowl of Middle Tennessee architecture.

By 1870, after the Ewells had brought the first jersey cattle into the Volunteer State from the Channel islands and developed the famous "Hal" strain of Tennessee Pacers, EWELL FARM had become a stockbreeding park of national acclaim. A later day visit here by another old soldier and lover of fine horseflesh, President "Teddy" Roosevelt, would add a final flourish to the historic panorama of the Ewell home's colorful past.

If together the Ewells had managed to climb above the poverty and despair of the Reconstruction South, so together, too, almost within hours of each other, death would beckon them to their last reward.

Today, with the same constancy of their eternal love, the Middle Tennessee sun shines through a stained glass window in Columbia's St. Peter's Church to lend a kind of Heavenly meaning to these words: "R.S.E., 1818-1872, L.C.E., 1820-1872—In their deaths they were not divided."

This magnificent window in Columbia's ST. PETER'S EPISCOPAL CHURCH memorializes the everlasting love of EWELL FARM'S most famous lord and lady.

61

McKISSACK HOME
1845
". . . like the Devil's own pitchfork . . ."

Spring Hill's McKISSACK HOME owes its special place in history to a Rebel cavalier with a bullet in his brain and a squatty little Yankee general, who hated to give up his sword.

Built in 1845 as the first brick house in Spring Hill, this fine old place was also the girlhood home of the notorious Jessie McKissack, a real flesh-and-blood Scarlett O'Hara of her day.

Sometime in the spring of 1863—after the vivacious Jessie had already said her marriage vows to Dr. George B. Peters—a darkly handsome Mississippian, Gen. Earl Van Dorn, had ridden into town and set up headquarters as commander of Confederate cavalry in Middle Tennessee.

Like the events that sired the war itself, no one can say just when the rumors about Jessie Peters and Earl Van Dorn actually began. All would end though with an abrupt finality in the thunder of a single pistol shot on May 7, 1863. The General, as he sat working at his headquarters desk, his back turned to an irate Dr. Peters, had his brains blown out in the fury of a tragic moment that even history has tried hard to forget. Fleeing the scene and escaping through the Union lines into Nashville, for a time George Peters became a self-styled hero as the slayer of "that infamous Rebel, Earl Van Dorn." He had no way of knowing then that Jessie, garbed in her widow's weeds, would one day stand over his own grave and mutter down at him, "I never loved George, but I guess I owe him this much."

If the saga of Jessie Peters and Earl Van Dorn had cost the South one of its most brilliant fighting men in the spring of '63, a year and a half later the spotlight of history would once again fall on the McKISSACK HOME and the humble little hamlet of Spring Hill, Tennessee. Scholars and students of military science and tactics are still scratching their heads in disbelief of the events that took place just south of town on the night of November 29, 1864. In one of the most mysterious phenomena of the entire Civil War, young, portly and bewhiskered Gen. John Schofield—outnumbered and almost completely encircled by John Bell Hood's Confederate Army of Tennessee—under the cover of darkness, managed to sneak his fleeing 22,000 Union soldiers across the entire front of Hood's slumbering veterans.

Even as his army creaked and groaned its way past his temporary headquarters in the McKISSACK HOME, the sentimental Schofield, still not convinced that he would make good his escape, prevailed upon the mistress of the house to leave his sword with her for safekeeping. The General was muchly relieved when Mrs. McKissack graciously obliged. To John Schofield, being captured was one thing; surrendering his blade to an old West Point classmate was quite another.

The next morning, as a furious Gen. Hood drove his tattered legions northward in pursuit of Schofield, few would have time to notice the long shadows of fall, shaped like the Devil's own pitchfork, that even today point an accusing finger at the girlhood home of Jessie McKissack.

HOMESTEAD MANOR
1819
". . . a woman has your flag!"

When Virginia-born Francis Giddens put the final flourish to HOMESTEAD MANOR in 1819, Thompson Station, Tenn., was bequeathed its most distinguished landmark.

Built at a time when foldaway beds were still a newfangled source of amazement and a closet in every upstairs bedroom was an undreamed-of convenience, HOMESTEAD MANOR was a house to lift even the most sophisticated brow. As a native son of the Old Dominion State, it comes as no surprise that Francis Giddens would borrow these unique innovations in his new home from historic MITCHIE TAVERN just outside of Charlottesville and within a stone's throw of Jefferson's MONTICELLO.

Situated between Spring Hill and Franklin on Columbia Pike, one of the main avenues of the Civil War in Middle Tennessee, HOMESTEAD MANOR will always remember the morning of March 5, 1863. Caught between Van Dorn and Forrest to the south and Col. John Coburn's Federals to the north, this old Williamson County house saw much of the five-hour-long Battle of Thompson Station literally fought in its yard.

If every battle in history has had its heroes and its cowards, few can boast a young heroine the likes of Alice Thompson, the seventeen-year-old daughter of Elijah Thompson, for whom Thompson Station was named.

Alice was on her way to a neighbor's house when the sudden crackle of rifle fire had sent her scurrying to join her friends, the Banks family, in the safety of their cellar at HOMESTEAD MANOR. There, in the gathering gloom of anxious anticipation, she watched as charge after charge of Rebel-yelling infantry rolled across the lawns outside, only to be hurled back bleeding and broken by the hard-fisted Yankees. Suddenly, when the guidon bearer of the Third Arkansas was shot through just outside her window, Alice Thompson rushed up the cellar steps, grabbed up his colors and waved them bravely above her head. "Look, boys," Col. S. G. Earle yelled at his wavering regiment, "a woman has your flag!" Inspired by this kind of instant courage on the part of a young girl and stung to new fury by their Colonel's words, the Razorbacks of the Third Arkansas turned and rooted a hole in the Yankee line that would have made even their namesakes proud.

Alice Thompson would die six years later at twenty-three, the wife of a young Rebel soldier who had fought that day at Thompson Station.

RODERICK
1815-1820
In memory of a horse

This Federal gem of a house was built by Spencer Buford after his 1801 marriage to Elizabeth Giddens of nearby HOMESTEAD MANOR. This old place stands on a portion of a 3,000 acre tract that had earlier cost his father the extravagant sum of $500. At seventeen cents an acre the elder Buford could well afford to give his son a handsome hilltop for his new home.

To say that the Buford family and their neighbors, the Giddens clan of HOMESTEAD MANOR, had an affinity for each other would be putting it mildly. Not only did Spencer Buford look across the road for his bride, so did his brothers, Charles and James. This matrimonial monotony was finally reversed when one of the Buford girls gave her hand in marriage to a Giddens son.

The two most outstanding features of Spencer Buford's new home were a handsomely recessed entrance doorway and unique corner fireplaces for better heat distribution and to enable a single chimney to serve two adjoining rooms. These unusual corner fireplaces remain a symbol of the warmth and hospitality that abound in this old house right down to the present day.

A daughter of Spencer and Elizabeth Buford, Amelia was the first wife of Dr. Elijah Thompson. When the railroad came through these parts in 1850, Thompson Station was named for this prominent physician, planter and State Legislator.

During the Civil War when Gen. Nathan Bedford Forrest's favorite mount, Roderick, was shot from under him in the Battle of Thompson Station, the dead horse was brought here for burial. Although his grave site is not known, this fine old Middle Tennessee house is today called RODERICK in honor of his gallant memory.

The corner fireplaces found at RODERICK are particularly unique.

BEECHWOOD HALL
1856
Hay on the stair and a truck in the hall

But for a generous purse and the rolled-up sleeves of deep devotion in our own time, BEECHWOOD HALL may well have tumbled unnoticed and forgotten into the ashes of the past. Instead, today, thanks to its present owners, Betty and Harry Morel, this grand old Williamson County house on Carter's Creek Pike can be proudly pointed to as one of the most courageous restorations in all of Middle Tennessee.

Built in 1856 by Henry George Washington Mayberry, BEECHWOOD HALL perches on what was then a beech tree covered kneecap of the surrounding Harpeth Hills, proof positive once again that matching the early Middle Tennessean's yen for fine horseflesh and sour mash whiskey was a strange obsession to raise his houses and his tombstones in lofty places.

Like Scarlett's beloved TARA, the great grove of virgin beeches has "Gone with the Wind" of change now and left BEECHWOOD HALL, iced white and gleaming, the sole ruler of long falling green pastures and unbroken breezes.

Today, it is hard to imagine that BEECHWOOD HALL—pegged and tongue-and-grooved together in the finest tradition of George Washington Mayberry's day—just a few short years ago clung to its last vestige of life on the Skid Row of abandonment and neglect. A survivor of that bitter era of defeat and Reconstruction, when what was left of the Old South was "too poor to paint and too proud to whitewash," BEECHWOOD HALL'S final hour of humiliation found hay molding on its magnificent free-standing stair, pieces of lumber poked through its gently arched windows, and an old farm truck unceremoniously dripping grease on the half foot thick heart pine floor of the great central hallway. Such was the challenge of BEECHWOOD HALL for Betty and Harry Morel.

It is hard to believe today that an old farm truck once dripped grease on the floors of this grand entrance hall and that a hundred slaves lined the elegant stairway to prove its strength when this fine old house was first built.

View from the upstairs balcony of BEECHWOOD HALL.

LAUREL HILL
1854
On the highway to history

Though its stately walls would tremble more than once at the distant sound of angry guns during the Civil War, LAUREL HILL survived it all to remain a cherished landmark of the Columbia-Franklin Pike.

If the earliest vitals of this old house reach all the way back to the early 1800's, a transplanted Kentuckian—James P. Johnson—is credited with the 1854 additions that make LAUREL HILL what it is today.

Although its double-decked entrance portico was the inspiration of a later time, this charming Williamson County manor house has been spared the flippant whims of change suffered by so many of its antebellum contemporaries. From the date of its completion it seems to have been the kind of house that to add anything would be to "gild the lily," and to take anything away would always be a crime.

Mellowed by its age and landscaped today in casual perfection, James Johnson's LAUREL HILL was once the nerve center of one of the most progressive plantations in all of Middle Tennessee. The fine blooded harness horses and purebred cattle that grazed these gentle meadows of yesteryear brought both a multitude of local admirers and many an eager purse galloping up the winding drive to partake of the ever genial hospitality of LAUREL HILL.

Hovering above the Civil War's main thoroughfare between Columbia and Franklin, this old place had a grandstand seat as history was being written in blood and desolation across these Harpeth Hills. Time and again, its latchstring lifted by friend and foe alike, LAUREL HILL was once a welcome sight to many a thirsty and hungry Billy Yank and Johnny Reb who will never pass this way again.

HARRISON HOUSE
Circa 1848
". . . a handsome metal coffin . . ."

Hanging on his crutch like a wounded crow, Gen. John Bell Hood clumped up the brick walk to William Harrison's white-pillared home in the early afternoon of Nov. 30, 1864. From this moment on the HARRISON HOUSE would have a special place in American history.

In the library of this famous old home, Gen. Hood issued the order that would begin the two-hour-long blood bath that was the Battle of Franklin. This same fateful Indian Summer's afternoon the front steps of the HARRISON HOUSE was the scene of flaring tempers between Hood and Gen. Nathan Bedford Forrest, Chief of Cavalry. Forrest favored a flanking movement over a frontal assault and said so in very colorful terms. Hood, with a short fuse of his own, raged back that he, and not Forrest, was the commanding general and that the Army would make the charge against Schofield. According to witnesses, the argument ended when Forrest stalked off to rejoin his troops.

Just two months earlier, a mortally wounded John H. Kelly had been brought up these very same steps to die on an early September day and be buried in a handsome metal coffin supplied by a group of grateful citizens of Franklin. As the youngest general in the Confederate army, Kelly had been struck down leading a charge of Wheeler's cavalry at nearby Parry Station. Ironically, this young hero is said to sleep today in an unmarked grave in his native State of Alabama.

If John Bell Hood had issued the order to begin the Battle of Franklin under William Harrison's roof, it would not take long for the blood and debris of the next two terrible hours to begin flowing down the Columbia-Franklin Pike.

Among the first of the wounded to be brought to the HARRISON HOUSE were Gens. William A. Quarles and John C. Carter. In time, Gen. Quarles would recover from a shattered left arm to wed his sweetheart back home. John C. Carter would linger on in agony until the Tenth of December, when he would breathe his last at twenty-seven, the youngest of six Confederate generals to give their lives at Franklin.

Still with us as it has been since it was built around 1848 by William Harrison, one-time High Sheriff of Williamson County, the HARRISON HOUSE will always be a special landmark in the imagination of those who have come to know and love the lore and legend of early Middle Tennessee.

It is believed that Gen. John Bell Hood planned the Battle of Franklin in this room of the HARRISON HOUSE.

RURAL PLAINS
Circa 1830
Legacy of a lonely brother

There were three things in life about which Buck Martin was always mighty proud. He had been a Colonel on General Jackson's staff at the Battle of New Orleans, built a fine Middle Tennessee house named RURAL PLAINS and stayed a bachelor all his days.

Col. Martin had transplanted himself from North Carolina to Williamson County around 1800. Before traipsing off with Jackson to fight the British in the War of 1812, he had built a comfortable little log cabin home near the site of present day RURAL PLAINS. This first house had served the bachelor Colonel well enough until he finally managed to convince a favorite sister, Sally Jane Hughes, and her husband, John, to leave Virginia and make their home with him in Middle Tennessee. This was around 1828. Two years later Buck Martin began building RURAL PLAINS to meet the growing needs of his newly found family.

For twelve joyous years Col. Martin shared his roof with Sally Jane and John Hughes and their children. Gone forever now were the days and nights of loneliness that had once plagued the earlier period of his bachelorhood.

When his sister died in 1842, Buck Martin, himself only one more year to live, shared the sadness of her distraught husband. So deep was John Hughes' grief that during his lifetime he would never permit the removal of his wife's steps from her side of the four poster bed they had shared since their wedding night. In this same bed, on the day after Christmas, 1860, John Hughes would come to his own tragic end. An invalid in his latter years, he had fallen into the fireplace in his room and been fatally burned on Christmas Eve. When discovered by the housemaid who brought in his supper that night, the pullcord that would have summoned help lay just beyond his unconscious fingertips.

WALNUT WINDS
Circa 1840
A barrel of sugar every Christmas

WALNUT WINDS is a humble little house richly steeped in the lore and legend of early Middle Tennessee.

Whipsawn out of logs of blue poplar and pegged into shape on Williamson County's Lewisburg Pike sometime around 1840, this old place has been many things to many people.

In its happier days before the Civil War it was the home of Dr. Hezekiah and Veturia Oden, the ill-fated parents of six little daughters. As a member of the Fourth Confederate Cavalry, Dr. Oden's death in 1864 had followed that of his wife the year before. This double tragedy had brought Mrs. Oden's sister, Mary Susan Reams, hurrying to WALNUT WINDS to care for her orphaned nieces who had been left behind on the mercy of the world.

When a wounded officer of Forrest's Cavalry was nursed back to health here in the closing days of the War, he would never forget Miss Mary Susan's many kindnesses in his hour of need. Every Christmas for the rest of her life, she would find a barrel of sugar waiting on her doorstep.

Two other Rebel soldiers who came this way during the War, Col. L. O. Williams and Lt. Walter G. Peter, did not fare so well. Legend has it that these two men stopped by WALNUT WINDS and were treated to a long overdue hot meal just the day before they were captured and strung up to the Hanging Tree in Franklin as spies on June 9, 1863. Col. Williams, a cousin of Gen. Robert E. Lee, was buried in a single grave with Lt. Peter. He still had his sweetheart's locket around his broken neck.

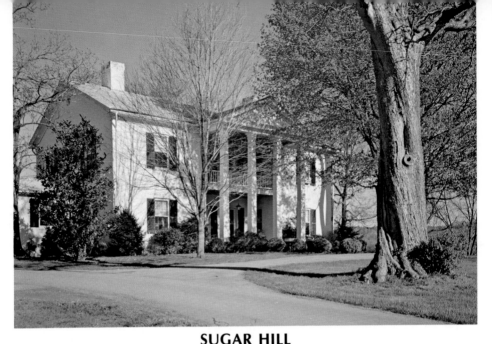

SUGAR HILL
After 1834
". . . across his own threshold"

Franklin Hardeman was a proud man who wore the courage of his convictions like a badge of honor all his days.

When Catherine Wilson became the fifteen-year-old bride of Frank Hardeman sometime in 1834, her father offered to build the young couple a fine Williamson County home as a wedding present. Although such a proposal was quite common in those days of Old South abundance, Franklin Hardeman could not accept this kind of generosity. To this youthful Middle Tennessean, if a man took on a new wife, he should be able to carry her across his own threshold.

Out of this kind of special pride and a plentiful purse of his own, Frank Hardeman raised the handsome brick walls of SUGAR HILL. Gazing proudly westward across the wayward wanderings of the Lewisburg Pike, this grand old manor house would take its colorful and unique name from the first Hardeman homeplace to be built in Williamson County.

The new master of SUGAR HILL was an offshoot of some of the hardiest stock ever to sink its roots in this section of early Middle Tennessee. Old Thomas Hardeman, Franklin's grandfather, had smelled British powder alongside John Sevier at King's Mountain during the Revolution. He had also been a delegate to Tennessee's first Constitutional convention and a senator in the new state's second General Assembly. Frank Hardeman's father, Peter, put together with the same kind of glue, had fought Pakenham's Redcoats at New Orleans in the War of 1812.

If two generations before him had given much to see this nation through the labor pains of its birth, Franklin Hardeman would offer no less as his country marched toward the graveside of Civil War in the late 1850's. Although he represented heavily secessionist Williamson County in the Tennessee Legislature, the master of SUGAR HILL soon made it plain that he planted his feet in the middle of his own beliefs—no matter how much mud splattered on his boots. As a died-in-the-wool Unionist, he took the view that whatever George Washington and Andrew Jackson had joined together, no man had a right to put asunder. True to this conviction throughout the War, many was the time a word from Frank Hardeman spared a neighbor the hard hand of the Yankee invader.

RIVERSIDE

Before 1843

From Old Hickory great cedars grew

The ancient cedar trees that line the lawns of RIVERSIDE are among this old Middle Tennessee house's most prized possessions.

When James Randal McGavock began looking around for a wife, once his eye fell on his first cousin, Louisa Chenault of Bardstown, Ky., he knew he need look no further.

Following their marriage on Nov. 1, 1832, the young newlyweds began building a brick plantation house on a bluff overlooking the Harpeth River. Located hardly more than a stone's throw from CARNTON, the new groom's childhood home, RIVERSIDE was still under construction when it hosted a most distinguished visitor.

Andrew Jackson and Randal McGavock, Sr., had been friends from Middle Tennessee's frontier days. When word reached THE HERMITAGE that Randy McGavock's boy was building himself a home on the banks of the Harpeth, Old Hickory had come jostling down to Williamson County with a carriageful of cedar saplings that he set out himself around the lawns of RIVERSIDE. Many of these old giants still stand today as lasting proof that one of the truly great Presidents of the United States also knew what he was doing when it came to planting cedar trees.

Louisa McGavock gave birth to ten children at RIVERSIDE. Although their father would die soon after the beginning of the Civil War, many of the McGavock offspring were still at home that fall afternoon in 1864 when the Federal guns of Fort Granger announced the opening of the Battle of Franklin. For two terrible hours of rattling windowpanes and trembling walls, every member of the family watched and waited with bated breath as the two armies struggled to their death across the river.

The RIVERSIDE of these earlier years is a far cry from the RIVERSIDE we know today. The transition from the unpretentious brick farmhouse of Randal and Louisa McGavock to the elegant Middle Tennessee country home of the present is the result of a fire early in this century.

Although the original walls and foundation were used in the restoration, four white pillars and a sweeping second story veranda were added to provide RIVERSIDE the grand demeanor this old house has always deserved.

CARNTON
Circa 1828
Five dead generals on a rear veranda

The peace of plenty and the trials of tragedy have both stalked the stage of historic old CARNTON.

Armed with the pocketknife of a fine Virginia background and honed by a Pennsylvania education in the whims of the Law, Randal McGavock wandered southwestward in 1796 to carve his name forever on the totem pole of Middle Tennessee history.

His rise to prominence began in the old Mero District where he soon elbowed his way into various and sundry minor judicial offices. Never one intended to be mired long in the lowly stations of life, by 1824 Randal McGavock was tipping his hat as the newly elected mayor of Nashville.

Just as his political star had been quick to rise, so would his financial fortunes. Shortly after 1825 his huge land holdings in Williamson County demanded that he pull up stakes in Nashville and move south to settle in the countryside near Franklin. If Randal McGavock was the kind of man to whom legends cling, rumor had it that a bulk of his Harpeth River properties were the result of a one-sided Indian trade for a pony and a second-hand shotgun. Whether true or false, none can say. That this ambitious Irishman was one of the most enterprising and shrewdest men of his day, no one can deny.

Since Rachel Jackson had a hand in helping Mrs. McGavock plan its magnificent formal gardens, CARNTON, named for the family's ancestral home in Ireland, was probably completed around 1828. In December of this same year, Rachel would die at THE HERMITAGE, less than three months before Randal McGavock's good friend, Andrew Jackson, would be inaugurated seventh President of the United States.

For fifteen tranquil years of peace and plenty, Randal McGavock would swing wide the doors of CARNTON to men like Jackson, Secretary of War John Eaton, Judge John Overton, Sam Houston and James K. Polk. Another frequent visitor was Senator Felix Grundy, Mrs. McGavock's distinguished brother-in-law who would also serve as Van Buren's Attorney General.

Even the grounds of CARNTON have been plowed and harrowed by history. As the thunder of Civil War ripped the nation apart in the spring of 1861, Co. H. of the

When the slaughter of the terrible Battle of Franklin was finally over, the rear veranda at CARNTON held the bodies of five Confederate generals.

Twentieth Tennessee Infantry threw out its chest and came to Attention for the first time in the shade of nearby McGavock's Grove. In its ranks, his hand upraised in allegiance to the Confederacy, was young Tod Carter. The peach fuzz of youth still soft on his cheek, this same Tod Carter would fight his way through three years of war, only to fall mortally wounded in the Battle of Franklin—within a stone's throw of his childhood home. Two weeks later, youthful Col. William M. Shy would fight what was left of the Twentieth Tennessee to fragments on the slopes of Nashville and be brought back to Williamson County for a hero's burial.

Randal McGavock died in 1843 and was followed by his wife, Sarah, eleven years later. Both were graciously spared the twilight aftermath of the Battle of Franklin, when the halls of CARNTON ran red with the blood of the two most tragic hours in American history.

John and Caroline Winder McGavock, its second master and mistress, were quick to volunteer their home as a hospital for more than 300 of the mangled and dying remnants of Gen. Hood's shattered army. Strung out on CARNTON'S back veranda that night, like a soiled row of discarded dolls, were the bodies of five Rebel generals who had heard their final bugle call—Pat Cleburne, H. B. Granbury, O. F. Strahl, John Adams and States Rights Gist.

Pat Cleburne and his four gallant comrades sleep elsewhere today, but the horrible nightmare of Franklin will be preserved forever at historic old CARNTON. At the rear of the house, separated from the rest of the world by a little iron fence, are two acres of headstones belonging to 1,481 Confederate dead, re-buried here from the battlefield by John and Caroline McGavock in 1866. Some say that the grass grows especially green in this place, that it is watered by the endless tears of the wives, mothers, sweethearts and children these brave men left behind.

Almost 1500 southern sons, fathers, sweethearts and husbands sleep beneath the sod of CARNTON'S Confederate cemetery. All had come to Franklin on the Indian Summer's afternoon of Nov. 30, 1864, to never go back home again.

RIVER GRANGE
Circa 1826
To help mend a broken heart

Five separate owners and four different names—this is about all that has changed about RIVER GRANGE in the last 150 years.

As the third in the grand parade of Perkins houses to be built on Del Rio Pike, this fine old home was a gift to a grief-stricken daughter from a kind and generous father.

In 1823 Mary Tate Perkins had married a Virginia cousin, Thomas Moore, and moved away to Arkansas to live. Two years later the Moores were back in Williamson County, accompanied by the tiny little coffin of their only child.

Col. Nicholas Tate Perkins was no stranger to this kind of tragedy. Blessed with the birth of fourteen children of his own, he was now down to his last surviving daughter. Though he could never mend her broken heart, perhaps a fine brick home nearby would somehow help Mary Tate and her husband pick up the shattered pieces and go on with life the way he and Mrs. Perkins had often had to do.

Just what prompted the bereaved couple to name their new home LOCUST VALLEY, no one can be sure. That they suddenly sold it to Daniel P. Perkins in 1867 under the terms of a somewhat unusual bill of sale is a matter of record. Mr. Perkins was allowed to buy their home and 338 acres of land on an interest-free installment basis. In return, he agreed to shelter the Moores, a niece of theirs and a favorite buggy horse at LOCUST VALLEY for the rest of their lives.

When Otey Walker bought this old place in 1889, it took on a new name—WALKER'S BEND. Later, it would be re-christened RIVER GRANGE at the suggestion of visiting Episcopal Bishop Charles Quintard, who could remember an earlier day when a golden sea of rippling wheat rolled across the lush bosom of this Harpeth River plantation.

A still later owner, Gen. Jacob McGavock Dickinson, would call this hospitable old home TRAVELLER'S REST, the same name Judge John Overton had long before bequeathed to his famous residence in nearby Nashville.

Once again pointed to as RIVER GRANGE by passersby on today's Del Rio Pike, any true lover of antebellum Middle Tennessee would have to hope that no more than the name of this old house will ever change.

TWO RIVERS
After 1810
In the backyard a hero lies.

Humbly erect—without frill or pretense—TWO RIVERS rises out of the shadows of the past with the quiet determination to remain forever a part of the present.

This old house was built shortly after 1810 by North Carolina-born Nicholas Tate Perkins—veteran of the War of 1812 and the Creek campaigns, prominent State Legislator and one of the instigators of Harpeth Academy. Following his 1790 marriage to his cousin, Ann, he would add to his other distinctions the fathering of fourteen children.

One of Nicholas Perkins' daughters, Marietta, was a girlhood friend of Adelicia Hayes of Nashville. Years ago, when the wallpaper was peeled from an upstairs bedroom, their names were found scrawled together on the plastering with the date, July 21, 1837. Neither girl had any way of knowing then that one day Adelicia would find herself the richest young widow in the whole United States.

William Shy was only ten years old when his father bought TWO RIVERS and moved his family here sometime in 1848. He had hardly grown to manhood when the thunder of Fort Sumter sent him off to war with the Twentieth Tennessee Confederate Infantry. He would no more than glimpse the light of his twenty-sixth year when the Battle of Nashville sent him home to TWO RIVERS and buried him beneath a humble headstone in the backyard of his youth.

Ordered to hold his ground at all costs in the face of overwhelming odds, young Col. Shy had been willing to pay the final price. He had fought his valiant regiment to pieces and died in its front to buy time for Gen. Hood to gather up the wreckage of his Army of Tennessee.

Shy's Hill in Nashville will always keep green the memory of this gallant soldier who sleeps ever so peacefully now beneath the sweet Middle Tennessee sod he gave so much to defend.

At the rear of TWO RIVERS stands a lonely marble headstone marking the grave of a young Confederate hero, Lt. Col. William Shy, killed fighting rear guard action for the Army of Tennessee at the Battle of Nashville. Shy's Hill is named in his honor.

77

MEETING OF THE WATERS
Circa 1810
First an enemy—then a friend

Handsome old MEETING OF THE WATERS would not be with us today but for an odd twist of fate.

When Thomas Perkins turned his back on his native Virginia and ventured into Middle Tennessee around 1800, the Redman still lay claim to this portion of Williamson County. Difficult as it was to find artisans with the skill to build a house like MEETING OF THE WATERS, it took even more doing to ask them to work with a trowel in one hand and a rifle in the other.

Nine years went into baking the brick, hewing the timbers and planing smooth the floors of MEETING OF THE WATERS—a fine old Georgian house that would have satisfied the most demanding Old Dominion appetite for pride and pretense.

Coincidence would play an early role in this household, when two of its daughters decided to wed two cousins. Both, oddly enough, were named Nicholas Perkins. One had earlier aided in the capture of the notorious Aaron Burr and personally seen to his delivery to the bar of justice in Washington City. With the death of his father-in-law in 1838, it was this Nicholas Perkins who would become the second lord and master of MEETING OF THE WATERS.

This same man would later oppose the marriage of his daughter, Margaret Ann, to handsome Robert Bradley on the pure and simple grounds that he was not a Perkins. Determined to squire his daughter off to the safety of an eastern boarding school, fortunately, he turned his back just long enough in Nashville to permit the young lovers to elope.

Another Nicholas Perkins, the third master of MEETING OF THE WATERS, would figure in a strange quirk of circumstance on the heels of the Battle of Franklin.

His right hand hopelessly crippled by a duel with a classmate during his old Centre College days, Nicholas Edwin Perkins was a pitiful match for the flotsam of Yankee marauders that spilled off the battlefield to rob and pillage his home. Told they planned to put MEETING OF THE WATERS to the torch once their haversacks were filled, he grabbed up a sword with his good left hand, sent his family off to safety in an upstairs room and planted himself defiantly outside their door.

Suddenly, there was a frenzied commotion below. From out of nowhere, a sabre-swinging Union officer had ridden up to the house and waded into the looters with a torrent of oaths that cleared the downstairs chaos within a few head-splitting moments.

Out of deepest gratitude and sheer amazement, Nicholas Edwin Perkins would extend his good left hand to this noble Yankee officer—the selfsame Centre College classmate who had put a ball through his good right arm so many years ago.

EVENTIDE
Circa 1840
Slave versus Master

EVENTIDE has to be one of Middle Tennessee's most remarkable restorations.

Originally known as WALNUT HILL, this proud old monument to the past, built sometime around 1840, was part of a 12,000 acre tract owned by colorful Nicholas Perkins. Famed for his part in the historic capture of Aaron Burr at the turn of the century, his will in 1848 left his WALNUT HILL property to the youngest of the Perkins daughters, Mrs. Nicholas Lafayette Marr.

Ironically, the Marr regime at WALNUT HILL would be marred by a tragedy that would do much to alter the legal landscape between master and slave in the State of Tennessee.

Ann was a fifteen-year-old Negro nurse of an infant daughter of the Marrs. To keep the baby quiet while she managed a nighttime rendezvous with another slave named Tom, Ann had given the child an unintentionally fatal overdose of laudanum. Convicted of murder by the Circuit Court of Williamson County, she was finally freed when this decision was overturned by the State Supreme Court on the basis of the young girl's ignorance of the dangers of the drug. A milestone had been reached, since the courts had found in favor of the slave instead of the master.

Years later another kind of tragedy was in store for WALNUT HILL. The tornado that struck the Forest Home section of Williamson County around 1918 left this old house in a state of disaster. This twister had torn away most of WALNUT HILL'S second story and flung its thirty-foot-tall Corinthian columns sprawling to the ground. Just who was able to make off with these giant pillars during this period of desolation and neglect is still a mystery. It is almost as big a mystery how the Claude Callicotts found the courage to undertake the restoration of this old house. By the time WALNUT HILL came into their hands in 1958, its ruins held out little hope that it could ever know again the elegant grandeur that had once been so much a part of its original heritage.

When the Callicotts' restoration was completed, this old place would have not only the new look of a full-width two-storied veranda and a new dignity but a new name—EVENTIDE.

MONTPIER
Circa 1821
To the bar of justice he brought Aaron Burr

Traitor or patriot? If the dictionary of history has never been quite able to define Aaron Burr, credit for the memorable capture of this dark son of intrigue must go to Nicholas Perkins, builder and first master of proud old MONTPIER.

Though the actual arrest of the notorious ex-Vice-President came at the hand of Capt. Edmund P. Gaines and took place in the early morning of February 19, 1807, it was Nicholas Perkins—young frontier lawyer and Major of Militia—who had first recognized the fugitive Burr at the Washington County home of a mutual friend the night before. Galloping off through the darkness to Fort Stoddart with his news, Maj. Perkins was on hand the next morning when Burr and a companion were overtaken near what is today the little South Alabama hamlet of McIntosh. A short while later, out of gratitude for his part in the capture of such a notable renegade, the youthful Major found himself with the 1,000-mile and often sleepless honor of escorting the wily Burr to the bar of justice in faraway Washington City. It has to be one of the real ironies of history that Nicholas Perkins, just two years previously, had been dispatched to the lower regions of the Mississippi Territory as Registrar of Lands by none other than President Thomas Jefferson, the one man Aaron Burr had loathed for so long above all others on this earth.

Today, hovering on a commanding rise above the Old Trace as it has for more than a century and a half, MONTPIER is still pointed to with a special kind of pride as the home of Nicholas Perkins—an adopted son of Middle Tennessee whose curious nature and keen eye helped slip the shackles of justice on a former Vice-President of the United States.

OLD TOWN
1842
Atop the cinders of the Ages

If OLD TOWN'S name is unique, so is its history.

Situated along the Big Harpeth River on the famous Natchez Trace, OLD TOWN stands on land once owned by John Donelson, one of Nashville's founding fathers. Over a thousand years ago this same tract belonged to an ancient tribe of highly advanced Indians. For generations now archaeologists have had a field day digging in the numerous mounds left here on the west bank of the Big Harpeth. The result has been definite proof that a large and well fortified village once covered this site. Since this was centuries before the first Christian missionary ventured this way, the two cross-shaped mounds in OLD TOWN'S front yard lend an even greater aura of mystery to this fine old Williamson County home.

When Virginia-born Thomas Brown completed OLD TOWN in 1842, he had his second wife. Three weeks after the death of the first Mrs. Brown had left him with two young sons to raise, Thomas married the widowed Margaret Hunter—his dead wife's best friend. Oddly enough, four children and thirty-two years later, Thomas Brown's final deathbed request in 1870 was to be laid to rest at the side of his first bride, Nancy.

In the meantime, the Civil War would pay more than one visit to OLD TOWN'S hearthstone. A son-in-law, John Bowman, would have an arm shattered at Atlanta, while the military service of a son, John Thomas Brown, would strangely parallel that of the heroic young Tennessean, Sam Davis. Like Sam, John Thomas had got his baptism of fire with the First Tennessee Infantry, been wounded at the Battle of Perryville and captured and imprisoned by the Yankees as a member of Coleman's Scouts. Here the parallel ends. John Thomas Brown lived to survive the Civil War, while Sam Davis was hanged at Pulaski as a spy.

Too old for service himself, Thomas Brown lived only five years after Appomattox. His health had been broken during the War's closing days in a Nashville prison for his refusal to take the oath of allegiance to the Union.

Across this old stone bridge near OLD TOWN Andrew Jackson marched his men down the Natchez Trace to fight the Battle of New Orleans during the War of 1812.

81

HARPETH PRESBYTERIAN CHURCH
1836
". . . the error of their ways"

Williamson County's HARPETH PRESBYTERIAN CHURCH stands on land donated by the Samuel McCutchen family as early as 1811.

Until 1836, when old Sam McCutchen's son, Robert, had his slaves fire the brick and saw to the building of the present sanctuary, the first HARPETH PRESBYTERIAN CHURCH was nothing more than a simple one room log cabin—as humble and plain as the faith of the little band of communicants that bowed its head in worship here so long ago.

As was the case with so many Middle Tennessee congregations before the Civil War, Sundays saw the doors of HARPETH PRESBYTERIAN CHURCH opened to slave and master alike. These were the days when sections of the surrounding churchyard were also used as a common burial place for members of both races as friends in Christ.

During the years of war that surged through these gentle hinterlands of the Little Harpeth River, the trail of blood, sweat and tears would often lead both armies across the threshold of this old Williamson County landmark. Fortunately, as if protected by some special Heavenly dispensation, HARPETH PRESBYTERIAN CHURCH came through it all, scarred only by its memories of those terrible days when Christian men of both sides sought to dig out the splinters of their differences with the point of a sword and paid a tragic price for the error of their ways.

BATTLE OF FRANKLIN
1864
The day five generals died

The BATTLE OF FRANKLIN has been called "The Gettysburg of the West." After what happened here in the lean shank of the afternoon of Nov. 30, 1864, it could also go down in history as "John Bell Hood's personal slaughter-pen."

If ever a fight was fought out of the fierce fury of one man's frustration and a whole army's determination to prove its mettle, such was the BATTLE OF FRANKLIN. Never before or since have so many brave men been asked to give so much to gain so little as in the sallow twilight of this terrible day. Seldom has so much hung on the hook of one man's judgment and so many died on the vine of unmatched valor for his lack of it.

Strung out two corps wide across the sloping shoulders of Winstead Hill, the Confederate Army of Tennessee would soon face the strange dilemma of being too weak to win and too proud to lose. Perhaps no army in history was worse led, worse fed, had a fiercer pride in its heart, no more ticks beneath its collar and no bigger fool in its front than the Rebel army of John Bell Hood that was getting ready to kill itself on an Indian Summer's afternoon in the sleepy little farming hamlet of Franklin, Tenn. Standing on no more than its pride, willing to give far more than it could spare, this army of lice and scarecrows would soon fight itself to death on the plains below out of one man's sheer foolhardiness and its own sheer guts to prove itself, once and for all.

By three o'clock it had become apparent to all that Gen. Hood had decided to swing the lean and angry fist of his Army of Tennessee against the well-fed and well dug-in jaw of John Schofield's sturdy Midwestern veterans. Within the next two furious hours more Americans would be killed and maimed than in any other two hours of this nation's history.

If the death knell of the southern Confederacy was already tolling, at the BATTLE OF FRANKLIN men of both sides seemed more prone to kill each other than listen. If raw courage ever had any more to say, it would never be said better than in this place. If John Bell Hood was dreaming dreams of military immortality, before this day was through the Southland he had given an arm and leg for would itself lay mortally wounded by the wayside. When it was all over, it was decided that 'White Pillars' must come tumbling down—that the BATTLE OF FRANKLIN would reach far beyond the graves of heroism and touch the salty paths of tears quietly shed by a whole generation of sweethearts and widows.

Right up to the last, two of the army's best generals, Bedford Forrest and Pat Cleburne, opposed a frontal assault on the Federal lines. Hood, still fuming over Schofield's escape the night before at Spring Hill, would have nothing less. His gallant Army of Tennessee, itself smarting under the sting of Hood's accusation that it had lost its stomach to fight in the open, would give him this and a whole lot more.

At four o'clock the attack order was given. The next two hours saw the Confederates hurl themselves at Schofield's men with the frenzied fury of thirteen separate charges that killed the attacking Southerners so fast the dead often could find no place to fall.

When it was all done, Hood had paid a terrible price. Counted among his more than 6,000 casualties were the lives of five of his ablest combat generals: Patrick R. Cleburne, States Rights Gist, John Adams, O. F. Strahl and H. B. Granbury. Brig. Gen. John C. Carter would also die later of his wounds.

That night, as the smoke of this afternoon of sound and fury still wafted up from the Hell that was FRANKLIN, young Capt. Tod Carter lay dying in the room of his birth at the CARTER HOUSE. Fighting his way past places like Chickamauga, Missionary Ridge and Atlanta, the gallant Capt. Carter—the peach fuzz of youth still on his cheek—had been mortally struck down within a stone's throw of the threshold of his childhood.

Even the House of God did not escape the ravages of THE BATTLE OF FRANKLIN.

Altar in ST. PAUL'S EPISCOPAL CHURCH in downtown Franklin.

CARTER HOUSE
1830
He marched home to die

Franklin's CARTER HOUSE, its hindquarters still shot full of holes, was immortalized in a sea of blood on the afternoon of Nov. 30, 1864. Around this old place American sons and fathers killed each other with a fierce fury and reckless abandon unmatched by any other two hours in this country's history.

Fountain Branch Carter had moved with his father to Williamson County sometime around 1809. Virginia-born and the sixth generation of his family in America, he had grown to manhood in this early section of Middle Tennessee. At twenty-six and well on his way as a merchant, part-time surveyor and dabbler in local real estate, "Fount" Carter took himself a June bride in 1823. Seven years later, on Columbia Pike just south of town, he built the story and a half brick house that the blood-spattered pages of the Civil War would never be able to forget.

By the time 1860 rolled around, Fountain Branch Carter could count among his blessings twenty-eight Negro slaves, an added net worth of $62,000, three sturdy sons and four fine daughters. Listed among his losses along the way was the death of his beloved wife, Mary, and five of their children.

Fort Sumter saw the three Carter boys—Moscow at thirty-six, Theodrick at twenty-one and eighteen-year-old Francis—hurry off to nearby CARNTON in May of '61 to be sworn in as volunteers in Co. H. of the Twentieth Tennessee Infantry. Col. Moscow Carter would be captured early in the War and paroled home to Middle Tennessee. Francis was shot down at Shiloh and discharged the following fall. Tod, the second of the brothers, would be captured at Missionary Ridge, rejoin the Army, finally fight his way back home and die in the arms of those who loved him most.

Entrance hall and stairway.

The first Yankee brigade to come prancing past "Fount" Carter's house in Franklin was on the day after Christmas, 1862, while Gen. Rosecrans was on his way to fight Bragg at Murfreesboro. Two years later, on Nov. 30, 1864—in the golden glow of an Indian Summer's afternoon—the War would come surging up Columbia Pike to pay the CARTER HOUSE a much more personal visit.

Early on the morning of this fateful day, when Confederate Gen. John Bell Hood learned of the Union army's escape the night before at Spring Hill, his fury knew no limits. Quickstepping his Army of Tennessee northward in pursuit, he was determined to crush Schofield's Yankees wherever he found them, at whatever the cost.

From the slopes of Winstead Hill, two miles south of Franklin, Gen. Hood found the Federal army, its 22,000 men dug-in in a long sweeping arc just below town. Just within their lines stood the CARTER HOUSE, soon to be stenciled forever on the walls of history for finding itself in exactly the wrong place at precisely the right time.

The four o'clock bugles of Hood's first assault found seventeen members of "Fount" Carter's household and a neighboring family of five hovered in the safety of the CARTER HOUSE'S stone cellar. Through one of the tiny windows in its south wall, Col. Moscow Carter and his sixty-seven-year-old father got a ground level view of the carnage that took place outside.

The spearhead of Hood's first attack hit the Federals between "Fount" Carter's cotton gin and his barn just west of the Pike. In a frenzy of tooth-and-claw hand to hand fighting, his ragged Rebels temporarily split the Union line and surged past the front door of the CARTER HOUSE, only to be met and thrown back by Col. Emerson Opdycke's determined Yankee reserves.

Before the day was done, twelve more waves of Hood's Army of Tennessee would sweep down from Winstead Hill to dash themselves to pieces around the CARTER HOUSE. Between the cotton gin and "Fount" Carter's barn across the road, four of the five Confederate generals to die on the field at Franklin would be

First floor bedchamber where Tod Carter may have spent the final painful hours of his young life.

86

The sitting room is much as it was when the Battle of Franklin raged around the historic CARTER HOUSE.

killed within this brief span of two city blocks. Of the six to be wounded, five were shot down along this sector of the Yankee lines.

By nine o'clock that night the Battle of Franklin had dribbled away to the crack of an occasional rifle and the pitiful groans of whole mountains of torn and bleeding flesh. Briefly, word would be brought to the cellar that Capt. Tod Carter lay mortally wounded among the darkened wreckage of Hood's army. Guided by his young son's commanding officer, Gen. Thomas B. Smith, "Fount" Carter, along with three daughters and a daughter-in-law, would find Tod lying on the battlefield, within a stone's throw of the house where he had been born. In a matter of hours, beneath the roof of his childhood home, Capt. Tod Carter, CSA, would breathe his last.

After decades of frustration in the halls of Congress to have the CARTER HOUSE recognized as a historic national landmark, 1951 saw this old place and its grounds purchased by the State of Tennessee for $20,000. This same year brought about the founding of The Carter House Association, which joined hands with the Tennessee Historical Commission to undertake the monumental task of restoration.

Although "Fount" Carter's cotton gin, corn crib and barn have disappeared along with the sloping shoulders of the Yankee breastworks, everything else is much the

same as it was on that day long ago when 42,000 men sought to kill each other here and left the scars to prove it. Opened daily to the public under the auspices of The Carter House Chapter of the A. P. T. A., this old place—visited by thousands annually—has been designated by the National Park Service "as one of four sites in Tennessee of major historical importance in the development of the United States."

Upstairs bedroom.

More than one Yankee trooper took refuge on the back gallery of the CARTER HOUSE during the worst part of the fight. Its south wall is still riddled with the bullet holes to prove it.

Rear view of galleries and a corner of the old kitchen.

OTEY-CAMPBELL HOUSE

1830's

In the thick of a fight

Franklin's OTEY-CAMP-BELL HOUSE has seen it all—from a dead Yankee trooper in the front yard to the humiliating whack of an auctioneer's hammer.

Bathed in the sunlight of early spring and rooted in the rich lore of the past, the OTEY-CAMPBELL HOUSE'S exact building date is unknown. Another unexplained mystery about this old place is the marked similarity of its interior proportions and woodwork with Randal McGavock's CARNTON. The indication seems to be that some of the same artisans had a hand in building both of these fine old Williamson County homes.

Randal McGavock had been dead five years when his niece, Sally McGavock of Virginia came to Franklin in 1848 as the forty-three-year-old bride of local merchant prince, John H. Otey.

If it was a little late in life to be taking the matrimonial plunge, Sally Otey obviously intended to emerge from this new venture at least as well off as when she went in. A Wythe County, Va., pre-ceremony marriage contract shows her to be a woman of considerable holdings. It also stipulated that all of her properties were to remain in her name, be it McGavock or Otey.

Sally's new groom had been married before, and when the newlyweds moved into their home on the corner of Adams Ave. and Margin St. two of John Otey's sons—Patrick and James—were pleased to find themselves with a mother again. Rescued from the drought of old maidhood just in the nick of time, Sally Otey would also show her appreciation as a loyal and faithful wife for the last sixteen years of her husband's life.

The Oteys were still living on the corner of Adams and Margin on April 10, 1863, when a Confederate regiment of Gen. Van Dorn's cavalry suddenly slammed into the Yankee Fortieth Ohio Infantry planted in the vicinity of their home. The melee was brief but furious and scattered dead horses and dead men up and down both streets in the trauma of its aftermath. The fight of this April day would also leave the blood of Rebel wounded staining the wide plank floors of the OTEY-CAMPBELL HOUSE and a weeping comrade bent in despair over the lifeless form of a Union sergeant in its front yard.

Just as tragedy had often come to call on this old place during the War, humiliation was waiting in the wake of Reconstruction. Due to a civil dispute between the now widowed Sally Otey and John C. Carter, Mrs. Otey's home and three acres of its grounds would be sold under the auctioneer's gavel in the fall of 1865 for the paltry sum of $4,300.

Fortunately for us all, recent decades have seen Franklin's OTEY-CAMPBELL HOUSE enjoy once again the charm and simple dignity that have always been its noble birthright.

MORAN-POPE HOUSE

Circa 1822
Fine furniture for Old Hickory

If the little town of Franklin has its own special flavor, such early Middle Tennessee heirlooms as the MORAN-POPE HOUSE is one of the reasons why.

Charles Moran was hardly 'dry behind the ears' when he left the family roof in North Carolina to strike out on his own. Wandering into Tennessee in search of an older brother, he eventually apprenticed himself to a cabinetmaker and learned his trade so well that one day he would build furniture for Andrew Jackson's HERMITAGE. In the meantime, he took himself a bride in 1816, set up his own cabinet shop in early Franklin and built himself a fine two story townhouse just off the Square around 1822.

One of the high-water marks in Charles Moran's life was a lasting friendship with none other than the great Sam Houston, destined soon for Texas fame. So close were these two men that Houston called on Mr. Moran to be one of his seconds in his controversial duel with Gen. William White. Charles Moran was also one of the few people to whom Governor Houston ever revealed the mysterious circumstances that veiled his 1829 divorce from his bride of only three months. Out of this lifelong friendship the Morans' third son would be christened Samuel Houston for the man soon to become Texas' greatest hero.

Through the years Charles Moran's Franklin townhouse has had a multitude of owners. Since 1896 it has remained in the family of Dr. Thomas A. Pope, a distinguished citizen and well-known dentist here for more than a half century.

MASONIC HALL
1823
Divine words and dying men

More history has been written beneath the roof of Franklin's MASONIC HALL than in any other public house in town.

Completed in 1823 as the ancestral home of Hiram Lodge No. 7, this handsome old Gothic building has played host to everything from pious frontier sermons to the Civil War groans of dying men. It has served as the holy sanctuary of a distinguished bishop and the council hall of Indian chiefs. It has felt Rebel spies crouching behind its granite battlements and the long lean shadow of one of our greatest Presidents falling across its historic threshold.

Though the state's first legalized lottery furnished the funds to raise these regal walls, this somewhat less than holy beginning seems never to have troubled two of the most devout Christian souls ever to wear The Cloth. Within the spacious hospitality of this old hall a youthful James H. Otey preached some of the sermons that would one day lift him into the chair of first Episcopal Bishop of Tennessee. Used from time to time as a temporary meeting place by every church in town, the MASONIC HALL can also remember a few years later when another great evangelist, the Rev. Alexander Campbell, had ridden into Franklin in the winter of 1830 with God's Word in his saddlebags and Hell-fire and Damnation on his tongue.

The summer before Rev. Campbell's visit, President Andrew Jackson had used this old meeting house on a far less righteous mission. Accompanied by Secretary of War John H. Eaton and Gen. John Coffee, he had come here on Aug. 17, 1830, to tell an important gathering of Chickasaw Indian chiefs that they must soon move beyond The Great River and give up forever the ancient hunting grounds of their forefathers.

Many of the older warriors, who met with Jackson at the MASONIC HALL that day, had served earlier with him at New Orleans. There, facing the British together in the swamps of Chalmette, they had proudly come to know him as Sharp Knife—their leader and friend. Now that there were no more Redcoats to fight, this same Sharp Knife had come to ask the Chickasaw to turn his back on the heritage of a hundred generations.

As far as the Indians were concerned, the only cheery note of their whole visit to Franklin was furnished by Peggy Eaton's piano. These were the days when the Secretary of War's home stood on the corner just north of the MASONIC HALL. During a recess in the negotiations Peggy's piano was rolled to the front porch where she played and sang for a time to a somewhat bewildered audience of be-feathered chiefs, mingoes and headmen.

The Civil War's Battle of Franklin saw both sides put the MASONIC HALL to good use. First, the Confederates perched atop its lofty battlements to spy on Union gun emplacements across the river. After the fighting was done the hall was commandeered as a hospital and found itself choked to the rafters with Northern wounded.

The 1912 restoration of Franklin's MASONIC HALL was most appropriately made possible by a reparations payment from the Federal government to cover damages suffered by this grand old edifice on one of the bloodiest days in our nation's history.

EATON HOUSE
Before 1811
". . . battle of the petticoats . . ."

The Eaton family home in Franklin was made famous by a distinguished adopted son of Tennessee and the tireless tongue of gossip.

Sometime around 1811 John Henry Eaton had moved his widowed mother from their native North Carolina, settled her comfortably in this prim little Federal townhouse and hung out his shingle as a young attorney of the Bar.

As talented as he was handsome, John Eaton began to climb the ladder of success at a time in history when only death and dysentery could keep a good man down. His first claim to fame, the completion of Maj. John Reid's unfinished "Life of Jackson," was enough to get him elected to the Senate and start him on his way.

It was during his freshman term in Washington City that Sen. Eaton first met Margaret O'Neil Timberlake, a somewhat tarnished young lady who would one day prove the female trauma of his public life.

John Timberlake's death at sea as a young naval officer aboard the Constitution paved the way for John Eaton to add new grease to the wheels of a romance the wagging tongues of gossip had already set in motion. Within eight months after Lt. Timberlake's convenient demise, his widow stunned Washington society by becoming Mrs. John Henry Eaton on New Year's Day, 1829. This single event would blow the lid off Andrew

Jackson's first Cabinet, tear Old Hickory's own family to shreds and help elect a shrewd New York Yankee the next President of the United States.

The first gun of the "battle of the petticoats" was fired when Jackson made Sen. Eaton his Secretary of War and Mrs. Eaton was promptly snubbed by other Cabinet wives. Even the President's own niece and White House hostess, titian-haired Emily Donelson, refused to regard Peggy Eaton as her social equal. Remembering how his own beloved Rachel had been maligned by his political enemies, a furious Old Hickory finally solved the famous "Eaton Affair" with a total house cleaning. Calling for the resignation of his whole Cabinet, Jackson decided to start afresh. His nephew and personal secretary, Andrew Jackson Donelson, and his reluctant wife, Emily, were temporarily banished back to Tennessee. John Eaton was also sent south as the new Governor of Florida. Widower Martin Van Buren, with nothing to lose and everything to gain, had championed Peggy's cause alongside Old Hickory. Van Buren had gladly turned his back on the office of Secretary of State to go forth as Minister to the Court of St. James to await Jackson's nod of approval as the next President.

John Eaton, later to serve his country as Ambassador to Spain, died in 1856 and left Mrs. Eaton a wealthy widow. In time, however, a wily young Italian dancing master had come along to take Peggy's hand and her money in a third marriage and run off with her granddaughter, another Margaret Eaton.

The prim little Federal townhouse in Franklin, where John Henry Eaton began his colorful career so long ago, is today, most appropriately, the home of a well-known local law firm.

A fall day in Franklin is a joy to behold.

WALKER-RIDLEY HOME
1832
The fingertips of fall

Perhaps the last two lines of John Keats' "Ode on a Grecian Urn" best describe the WALKER-RIDLEY HOME in Franklin.

As one of three fine Walker houses to be built in the neighborhood of Fourth Ave. N. and Bridge St., the I's seem to have gone undotted and the T's uncrossed as to the details of this old place's early origins.

When, however, the erect and simple dignity of the WALKER-RIDLEY HOME is touched by the flaming fingertips of a fall day in majestic Middle Tennessee, we have to agree with Keats:

> ". . . Beauty is truth, truth beauty"—that is all
> Ye know on earth, and all ye need to know."

BOXMERE
After 1854
A day of blood, sweat and tears

During the Battle of Franklin, BOXMERE found itself just within the Federal lines. When Gen. Hood's Confederates decided to make a fight of it south of town, the Yankees set up brigade headquarters here for Gen. William Grose.

Although BOXMERE'S widowed owner, Mrs. Thomas Hardeman Figuers, and her two little daughters had fled to the safety of a nearby friend's house, two of her young sons and their dog, Fannie, stayed behind, entranced by the feverish activity of jangling spurs and rattling sabres. Later that afternoon the deep-throated roar of Fort Granger's cannon would send youthful Harden Perkins Figuers shinnying up the old yellow poplar at the back of the house for a bird's-eye view of the bloodiest two hours in American history. Years later he would recall how the cranky crackle of Rebel rifle fire had finally driven him from his lofty perch and into the cellar with Fannie and his brother, Tom. As the bullets whined into BOXMERE'S backside above their heads, littering the backyard with fallen Federals, a cannonball suddenly slammed into an overhead sill and sent both boys scurrying up to the first floor. By now the house was crawling with captured Confederate wounded and no doctor anywhere to be found.

Their own fright suddenly drowned by the sea of agony and blood that swirled about them, both boys bravely rolled up their sleeves and went to work building fires, hauling water and tearing up sheets and pillowcases for bandages. When young Harden Perkins ran downtown in search of a local physician, he returned to BOXMERE in dejected disgust. The doctor had refused to leave the safety of his office and venture into the streets. Later in the evening both boys were much relieved at the sight of their mother who, during a lull in the fighting, had hurried home to find her young sons and do what she could for the wounded and dying men.

More than a generation later several unexploded cannonballs would be unearthed beneath the lone surviving boxwood that lent BOXMERE its unusual name. Such were the grim mementos of a day of sound and fury this grand old place will never be quite able to forget.

McEWEN HOUSE
After 1842
A cannonball at suppertime

The historic Battle of Franklin paid a very personal call on the McEWEN HOUSE. It came here, announced by the thunder of a cannonball. It left with a trail of blood, death and a brand new five-dollar bill for four young angels of mercy.

The plot on which the McEWEN HOUSE stands today was once part of the great Williamson County land empire of Randal McGavock, the crown prince of CARNTON.

The oldest part of the house was put here around 1832 by one Carey Allen Harris— publisher of his own newspaper at fifteen, chief clerk of the War Department at twenty-eight, and acting Secretary of War for twenty-one days in the Cabinet of President Andrew Jackson.

When title to these premises passed to John B. McEwen sometime in 1842, the two-roomed bungalow of Carey and Martha Harris was almost immediately transformed into a stately Renaissance town house. Here would echo the first-born cries of five McEwen children—an only son and four lovely daughters.

Although the most vicious fighting of the Battle of Franklin took place around Fount Carter's house several blocks away, the McEwens of Fair St. would get their own bitter taste of the fierce fury of that twilight autumn afternoon—Nov. 30, 1864.

At the first bellowing defiance from the Union guns across the Harpeth River, all but one member of the McEwen household scurried below to the safety of the cellar. Mumbling indignantly that she still had the evening's meal 'to git un' with, an old Negro mammy had remained upstairs in the kitchen, loyally stirring her simmering kettles. It took the slamming of a Yankee cannonball into the McEwen smokehouse to send her 'skirts a-flyin'' down the cellar steps, thoroughly convinced at last that supper might just be a little late tonight.

During the worst of the fighting the population in the basement swelled with an unusual conglomeration of frantic neighbors, stray dogs, cats and Yankee soldiers. That night an endless stream of wounded from both sides surged across the threshold of the McEWEN HOUSE to cram every room and hall with bleeding, dying men. Though the Union casualties were the first to come, the color of a man's tunic made no difference in the tender mercies and kindly care extended by Mrs. McEwen and her daughters. For this gracious and gentle treatment of their fallen comrades, when the Yankees pulled back out of Franklin later that night, they left each of these gallant young ladies with a brand new five-dollar greenback of their eternal thanks.

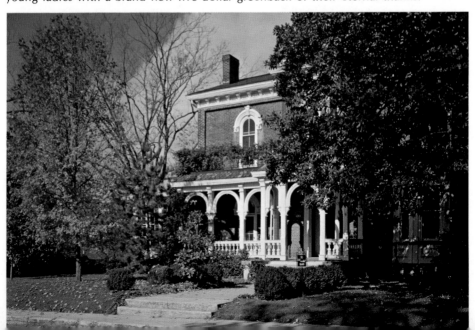

MAGNOLIA HALL
1840
Reflections of beauty

From the delicately laced crown of its widow's walk to the priceless collection of its antique furnishings, MAGNOLIA HALL is every inch a ruling queen in the regal court of antebellum Middle Tennessee.

Built in 1840, this rare heirloom of the Old South's Golden Age was once the pride and joy of Scottish-born William S. Campbell, one of Franklin's most successful early businessmen. As a man of mountainous means and hard-headed Irish determination, Mr. Campbell was the first president and guiding spirit in the founding of the first national bank to open its doors in Middle Tennessee on the thin heels of the Reconstruction era.

With its double-decked front verandas, gently arched windows and doorways, MAGNOLIA HALL brings to these hard-knuckled Tennessee hinterlands more than one trademark of that life so leisurely lived in the old mansions of the cotton and rice-rich downriver Mississippi and Louisiana lowlands. The most spectacular interior feature of this old house has to be the identical twin stairways that rise ever so gracefully from the central hallway to the second floor. Their perfect proportions and gentle ascent are sheer wonders to behold.

Owned today by a nationally recognized connoisseur of fine antiques and interior design, MAGNOLIA HALL, in this modern age, has ably adapted itself in the dual role of casual home and bountiful treasure chest of all things beautiful.

Its reflection ever painted like an everlasting portrait in the pond at the rear of the house suggests that even nature itself seems determined to extoll forever the regal charm of this grande dame of Middle Tennessee homes.

Twin stairways rise from the first
floor splendor of MAGNOLIA
HALL. Perfectly matched to the last
detail, they are an outstanding
trademark of this grand old house.

Dining room at MAGNOLIA HALL.

A visit in the drawing room
at MAGNOLIA HALL
is an experience long
to be remembered.

MYLES MANOR
Circa 1840
Forbidden to cross the river

With a flaming flourish of glory here and a stroke of golden grandeur there, MYLES MANOR is painted into a panorama of unbelievable beauty by the itinerant artistry of autumn in Williamson County.

So perfectly and tenderly cared for today, it is hard to imagine that this old place has housed the ups and downs of life for generations.

If the first years of the Civil War saw MYLES MANOR mourn the death of its builder and first master, Maj. William Maney, the Middle Tennessee rains had hardly melted the mound of his grave when new troubles came knocking at the door of his widow.

Once a son and grandson defied the Union authorities by wading the Harpeth River and slipping beyond the Yankee lines that girdled the town, Martha Murfree Maney, the sixty-two-year-old mother of thirteen children was hastily arrested at her home. When proved that she had given her 'tongue-in-cheek' nod to the boys' daring escapade, the widow Maney and her venturesome offspring were put under a $15,000 bond. Under no circumstances were they again to cross the Harpeth without written permission from Federal headquarters. Kept in this kind of military quarantine for some eighteen months after their arrest, these three members of the Maney household must have been much relieved when General Hood's boys finally rooted the Yankees out of town on the last day of November, 1864.

Like so many of Franklin's old homes, MYLES MANOR was used as a hospital by both sides during the Civil War that bathed the tranquil beauty of this Middle Tennessee hill country in a swirling sea of blood, death and destruction.

In more recent years, after a time as a private country club, MYLES MANOR has been returned to its rightful heritage as a home. Today, for all who will take time out to stand in awe of this old house and sip the sweet flavor of its secluded world, MYLES MANOR will always have a special place in every heart that comes this way.

TRUETT PLACE
Circa 1846
A bird's-eye view of Hell

Franklin's TRUETT PLACE has a double-barreled claim to a special kind of fame all its own.

This fine old house was built around 1846 by Alpheus Truett, a young nurseryman who had transplanted himself from Hickman County to Franklin a few years earlier. Just south of his homesite he had already set up the greenhouses that today establish Truett Floral Co. as the oldest continuing florist business in the entire State of Tennessee.

Alpheus Truett's fondness for good dirt under his fingernails had come early in life. His father before him had planted a fruit orchard on his Hickman County farm back when Tennessee had hardly more than climbed out of the wilderness and into the cradle of statehood. Thanks to a son and granddaughter who followed in his footsteps, Truett Floral Co. stayed in the family all the way to 1969—a span of some 125 years.

A far more imposing claim to fame than this, however, was bestowed on the TRUETT PLACE by Union Gen. John M. Schofield when he commandeered this white-pillared home as headquarters during the Battle of Franklin. At the same time the nearby greenhouses were taken over as a pay station for the Yankee troops who had been scurrying northward up the Franklin-Nashville Pike since early dawn.

Long years after he had taken up the reins of the family business Edwin Campbell Truett liked to pause from time to time above his endless rows of pots and sprawling ferns to recall the events of Nov. 30, 1864—the most unforgettable day of his life. Barely turned fourteen at the time, he could remember Gen. Schofield and his staff hurrying up the stairs to the south balcony as soon as news reached the house that Gen. Hood's boys had been sighted on the slopes of Winstead Hill, looking lean and hungry and ready for a fight.

Remembering how you could have cut the silent tension on the balcony like a warm piece of butter, young Truett was shoved brusquely aside when he had sought a boyish peep through one of the officer's field glasses. Then, just as Hood swung his distant Confederate brigades into battle formation, the kindly Schofield himself handed over his own binoculars and urged the lad at his side to have a good long look. Never, the General said, would he ever have the chance again to witness such a magnificent spectacle.

As the first cottonballs of smoke thundered from the throats of the Federal cannon across the river, the greenhouses and rows of shrubbery below the balcony were turned into a bedlam of shattering glass and trampling hooves. In a mad frenzy of activity the Yankee paymasters crammed freshly cut stacks of greenbacks into hiding beneath Mr. Truett's flower pots and made a mad dash for their horses. That night when the fighting was done they had returned to hastily retrieve their treasure. Fifty-one years later the Truett family would receive a Federal check for $395 to cover the havoc of their visit.

Sprung as it was from the gentle fountainhead of one man's quest for beauty, the TRUETT PLACE had been destined to have its special niche in history carved out forever by the hard hand of war.

100

WYATT HALL
1800
Where time stands still

WYATT HALL is one of those rare early Middle Tennessee little gems that has gone untouched by the wand of time and change.

Begun in 1797 and completed three years later, this real treasure of a place goes back to that day when the bricks for its perfectly patterned walls of Flemish bond were burned on the place by the slaves, and their masters thought of building their houses only one room deep. Since this was the style employed AT WYATT HALL all but one of its first floor rooms has the unique convenience of opening directly onto the unbelievable charm of its rear gardens. Again, with one exception, each of these rooms, along with their second story counterpart, has its own wood-burning fireplace that is still very much in use today. The mantel of one of these fireplaces is especially handsomely carved in a book and dentil motif to further complement the graceful dentil work found above the cabinet doors throughout the house.

Floored above and below with inch and a half yellow poplar planking, WYATT HALL'S upstairs rooms uniquely have ceilings one and a half feet higher than those at the entrance level. Beneath the house in three of its cellar rooms can still be found the original-old dirt floors.

For strength and protection against the everyday hazards of its frontier birth, all exterior walls are of solid brick, while the inside partitions are smoothed with a concoction of sand, lime and hog's hair.

Two of WYATT HALL'S original dependencies, an old log smokehouse and storage shed, still hover in quiet humility in the long falling shadows at the rear of the main house. Nearby, an ancient spring still bubbles forth from the lush bosom of these Middle Tennessee heartlands to furnish WYATT HALL'S water supply the way it has for more than 175 years.

Handmade wooden lock one of the many conversation pieces at WYATT HALL.

Old smokehouse and office at WYATT HALL.

The patriotically patterned draperies in
WYATT HALL'S parlor once hung in the
home of Dr. Samuel Mudd. It was Dr.
Mudd who set the broken leg of John
Wilkes Booth, the notorious assassin of
Abraham Lincoln.

Old kitchen at WYATT HALL.

The upstairs and its trundle bed
are typical of the early
heritage of this old house.

This medical chest belonged to Gen. John
Bell Hood's personal physician during the
Civil War. The rifle was carried by the
present owner's grandfather at the Battle of
Franklin. The old Slave Jug is also especially
interesting.

ASPEN GROVE
1834
When Andy Jackson got his nickname

The true beauty of ASPEN GROVE lies in its humble simplicity. Conceived in the fertile womb of Middle Tennessee's first beginnings, this old house has hugged the east shoulder of the Franklin-Nashville Pike for almost 150 years. With a special kind of Stoic serenity ASPEN GROVE has viewed the comings of the decades and the goings of men with an austere assurance that its simple charm would grow ever more pleasing beneath the mellow mantle of time.

Boasting none of the many splendored fineries of such nearby neighbors as THURSO and ASHLAWN, ASPEN GROVE was the pride and joy offspring of a particular moment in history. Here the son of a frontier blacksmith had stretched his ambitious legs from the dog trot front porch of his childhood to a fine new brick house all his own.

ASPEN GROVE, dating back to 1834, was built by Christopher Ervin McEwen, erstwhile young border captain turned prosperous planter in his middle years. Reared in youth behind the stockades of old Fort Nashborough, Christopher McEwen's feet had been planted early along the path to manhood. As a young militia officer he and his company of Tennessee Volunteers had followed Andrew Jackson 2,000 freezing miles downriver in the ill-fated Natchez Expedition of 1812-13. Frustrated at finding no one to fight and half starved by the long march home, Capt. McEwen had been on hand that memorable day in the trackless wilderness when an admiring soldier in the ranks had dubbed the General with his immortal sobriquet—Old Hickory.

After service again under Jackson—this time against the Creek Indians of the old Mississippi Territory—Christopher McEwen came home from the wars in 1815 to capture the hand in marriage of Rebecca Brown, a prominent Giles County belle of her day and sister of Tennessee Gov. Aaron V. Brown. Sadly, however, fate decreed that Rebecca McEwen not live to see the building of ASPEN GROVE. Instead, it remained for a second Mrs. McEwen, the former Narcissa Newsom, to become first mistress of the manor.

Named for the aspen poplars Christopher McEwen scattered over the grounds of his new Williamson County estate, ASPEN GROVE somehow managed to survive the wrath of four years of Civil War sloughing up and down the Franklin-Nashville Pike. Although those tragic days of hell and haversacks have long since trekked over the hills of the past, there still lingers about this noble old house the legend of a secret panel in a hall closet that afforded more than one southern son the right and freedom to fight another time on other fields in far distant places.

103

THURSO

Circa 1840

Because Sherman went to Georgia

THURSO has not always been as grand and elegant as it is today. Not too many years ago this fine old house stood forlorn and hollow-eyed just beyond the hustling, bustling world of the Franklin-Nashville Pike.

Had Mr. and Mrs. John Oman, Jr., not come along when they did, one of the most regal antebellum mansions in Middle Tennessee may well have been swallowed up by the subtle appetite of abandonment and neglect. Not only would the Omans give this stately old place a new beginning; they would also give it a new name—THURSO, in honor of the family's Old World origins in Scotland.

When THURSO was built around 1840 by James Johnston, the original house was devoid of the white-pillared, handsomely pedimented north and west porticos that have become its hallmark of elegance today. In Johnston's time there was a slimly columned, one story veranda—far more humble and so very typical of the slower paced, rocking chair world of early Middle Tennessee.

Happily, for such great old houses as THURSO, ASHLAWN next door and MOUNT-VIEW across the way, Gen. Sherman decided to march through Georgia with his flaming torches and leave the fate of these Tennessee hinterlands to the much more kindly hand and benevolent heart of Union Gen. John M. Schofield. What one destroyed at the pinnacle of four years of anger, another spared to be cherished and loved through the Ages.

MOUNTVIEW

Circa 1861

Out of the north rode an ex-preacher man

Proud and stately old MOUNTVIEW can look over the shoulder of the past and remember when 'The Man Who Came to Dinner' overnight became its second master.

If Old South abundance had furnished Buck Davis the pride and pocketbook to build himself a fine plantation house like MOUNTVIEW, this old place would be one of the lastborn of its noble antebellum brethren. The paint had scarcely dried on its great white pillars when the ebb and flow of Civil War up and down the Franklin-Nashville Pike served tragic notice that the clock was even then striking twelve on the glittering fairy tale of the South's Golden Age.

Raised on the brink of catastrophe and spared by the fickle whims of four years of marching armies, MOUNTVIEW was destined to suddenly change hands at war's end in one of the most unique real estate deals in all of Middle Tennessee history. It all began in the shivering twilight of a fall afternoon in 1865, when an ex-preacher man from up Smyrna way, Ashley Rozell, rode up to MOUNTVIEW'S gate in quest of a hot evening's meal and the shelter of a friendly roof for the night.

Later, as he gratefully shoved his chair back from the hospitality of Buck Davis' table, Ashley Rozell casually announced that he was on his way down to Franklin to consider the purchase of a plantation. MOUNTVIEW'S guest was in for a shock, however, when his host, with the casual manner of one accustomed to split-second decisions, suggested that they get their heads together on an agreeable figure and buy MOUNTVIEW instead.

If by the next morning Ashley Rozell had become the new owner of MOUNTVIEW in somewhat of an unusual manner, the second master of MOUNTVIEW was somewhat of an unusual man. Sprung out of the fountainhead of devout French Huguenot beginnings and prodded by the urgings of a Heavenly Hand, Ashley Rozell had been led in early life to serve his Maker as a leather-pounding fire and brimstone Middle Tennessee circuit rider. Along the way he had allowed himself the earthly fruits of three wives, nine children, and the accumulation of considerable holdings in Texas, Arkansas, and Memphis.

Though Ashley Rozell had retired from the active ministry at the time of his first visit to the house that would become the home of his final twenty-one years of life, he would leave the fingerprints of his deep Huguenot devotion on all that he touched in the Brentwood area of Nashville.

ASHLAWN
Circa 1836
A threshold of tears

The history of the first family of magnificent ASHLAWN reads like a Shakespearean tragedy.

This splendid old landmark of the Franklin-Nashville Pike was built by Richard Christmas about four years after his 1832 marriage to Mary Emeline Smith. The 200 acre ASHLAWN track had come down to the young couple as part of a Revolutionary land grant to Mary Emeline's maternal grandfather, Capt. James Leiper.

Killed by the Indians at the Battle of the Bluff, April 2, 1781, the Captain never saw the unborn daughter who would grow up to become the mother of ASHLAWN'S first mistress, Mary Emeline Christmas. A freak accident would also claim the life of Capt. Leiper's young widow. The grandmother of Mrs. Christmas would die at twenty from an exploding rifle that fell from its rack in her log cabin home in old Fort Nashborough.

Strangely, the bizarre pattern of tragedy that had claimed the lives of her grandparents would follow Mary Emeline Christmas to ASHLAWN. Richard, Jr., a baby son, would die here in 1837. Another son, William, on a trip away from home with a guide and his saddlebags stuffed with a large sum of money, mysteriously disappeared from the face of the Earth and was never heard from again.

As colorful and impulsive as he was wealthy, Richard Christmas suddenly announced one day in 1839 that he was selling ASHLAWN. Two years later he died and was spared the grief of knowing that his wife would be killed in a matter of months in a Mississippi River steamboat accident.

Despite such a history of trial and tribulation in the lives of its builder and first family, ASHLAWN, raised at the knee of Old South splendor, has been true to that heritage right down to the present day.

Walled-in on every side by thirteen inches of handmade brick burned on the place, the interior of this old house bears a striking resemblance to that of THE HERMITAGE. From its time-mellowed floors of ash and yellow poplar to its majestic free-standing stairway—handrailed and spindled in solid cherry—the inside world of ASHLAWN is a sight to behold.

Still unlocked by British brass from Carpenter & Company of London, each of the heavily paneled doors of its twenty-foot-square rooms is pegged together with a patient pride in craftsmanship and quest for perfection that has become a stranger to this day of hurried-up mass production and lack of elbowroom.

GREEN PASTURES

Circa 1840

A firing squad for an insult

GREEN PASTURES, as its name implies, is the lordly ruler of a pastoral world of peace and plenty all its own.

Pure Georgian in demeanor and manicured to perfection, GREEN PASTURES was built around 1840 under the watchful eye of that early Middle Tennessee master craftsman Asa Vaughn. Originally christened HADLEYWOOD by its first master and mistress, Denny Porterfield and Elizabeth Smith Hadley, this old place stands on a portion of a posthumous land grant to Mrs. Hadley's maternal grandfather, Capt. James Leiper—Nashville's first bridegroom.

Kentucky backwoodsman, a signer of the famous Cumberland Compact, and Revolutionary veteran—Capt. Leiper had died of Indian wounds in the long since spring of 1781. It had been fate's cruel decree that the good Captain never lay eyes on the unborn daughter who would one day become the mother of the first lady of GREEN PASTURES.

During the Civil War, having sent her own sons off to the sound of distant drums, GREEN PASTURES was destined to play host to friend and foe alike. As the years of sound and fury echoed among the surrounding Harpeth Hills, Bedford Forrest's Rebel cavalry troopers more than once pitched their tents on the sloping shoulders of these friendly acres. Later, on the heels of Hood's disastrous defeat at Nashville, the enemy—flushed with the intoxication of victory—swarmed out of his fortifications in the city and overflowed down the pike toward GREEN PASTURES.

While their home was being commandeered for a time as a hospital for Union wounded, the Hadleys were gratified to learn that even in the bitter gall of war the flower of chivalry blossomed on both sides of the Mason-Dixon Line. In a certain unfortunate instance an unnamed Yankee private was ordered before a firing squad by his commanding officer for his profane language and arrogant treatment of Mrs. Hadley.

Today, the whirlwind of war having spent itself against the far distant hills of yesteryear, GREEN PASTURES languishes on the sidelines of its own serenity and quietly shuns the hustle and bustle of the other world that lies beyond.

*Gateway to
GREEN PASTURES.*

107

MOORELAND

After 1838

". . . a silver pitcher of thanks . . ."

The Civil War saw the blood of the wounded of both sides stain the floors of MOORELAND. Those were the days when some of the fiercest fighting of the War was being fought out in Middle Tennessee's hilly heartlands, and Billy Yank and Johnny Reb took turnabout using this fine old Williamson County house as a hospital.

MOORELAND, reaching tall into the early twilight of a fall afternoon, can lay claim to some twenty-eight rooms and a unique history all its own.

With its somewhat unusual square-pillared front, hugged on either side by a low flanking wing, MOORELAND was begun by Robert I. Moore shortly after his father's death in 1838.

Robert Irvin Moore, like his house, was somewhat of an unusual man. Married to three wives in the span of his lifetime, he had fought the Indians under Jackson in his early years, made a fortune on the Square in Nashville as a middle-aged merchant and once received a silver pitcher of thanks for collecting a bad debt for some friends in Philadelphia. Unfortunately, death would claim Robert Moore before he would have a chance to finish MOORELAND as we know it today.

During the Civil War a fourteen-year-old son of Mr. Moore, Hugh Campbell, climbed out of a front bedroom window of this house one night and ran away to fight the War out in the Second Tennessee Infantry—despite his commanding general's promise to send him back home with a whipping for sneaking off before he was 'dry behind the ears.'

This same hard-headed Hugh Campbell Moore would grow up to sire six children at MOORELAND and live to see three of them die and be buried in the "second summer" of their infancy. Three sons would survive to prosper and take their rightful places among the prominent families of Williamson County.

WINDY HILL

After 1825

Children by the dozen

Strung along the shoulders of Old Smyrna Road are four everlasting monuments to a very special breed of men. One of these is WINDY HILL, once the home of Maj. Constantine Perkins Sneed.

If Constantine Sneed could trace the New World beginnings of his family all the way back to 1635 Virginia, the good Major could also point with pride to the fact that he had fought alongside Jackson at New Orleans in the War of 1812. At a later day he would send two sons to serve the Confederacy and die of a broken heart when one did not return.

Patriotic to the point where their family's name has figured with prominence in every single war of this nation's history, the Sneed men of Old Smyrna Road also had a special knack for siring children by the dozen. The builder of WINDY HILL was himself the eldest son of James and Bethenia Sneed's twelve offspring. In turn Constantine Sneed would father thirteen children of his own. Scarcely to be outdone, his youngest brother Alexander, the master of nearby FOXVIEW, would follow suit with twelve children born of his marriage to pretty Elizabeth Guthrie. In a period when giving birth for a woman was somewhat like playing Russian Roulette, there is good reason to believe that the Sneed women of Old Smyrna Road were of the same sturdy stock as the men who asked for their hand.

None can be sure of the exact building date of WINDY HILL. It is thought, however, that Maj. Sneed raised the walls of his house on a parcel of his father's 640-acre tract sometime shortly after he and Susannah Hardeman said their marriage vows in 1825.

Fortunately, Susannah Sneed would not live long enough to see the very heart torn out of what had always been to her the ever happy world of WINDY HILL. Four years after her death her husband would have to share alone the bitter news that Constantine, Jr., had been mortally wounded in the field at Chickamauga. She could never know that another soldier son, James Hardeman, would make his way through enemy lines to bury his brother in a casket of weathered boards, ripped from the sagging shoulders of an old barn in faraway north Georgia. So was Susannah Sneed spared the deep sorrow that all too soon brought her husband to her side in the little family burial plot along Old Smyrna Road.

FOXVIEW
Circa 1835
**Children and cousins
by the dozens**

The Sneeds of Old Smyrna Road had at least three things in common. They believed in marrying strong, healthy women, building fine houses and filling them to the rafters with their offspring.

The founder of the clan in this section of Williamson County, James Sneed, set the pace when he moved to Middle Tennessee from Virginia, built the family home on Old Smyrna Road and fathered himself twelve children by his first wife, the former Bethenia Harden Perkins.

James Sneed's eldest son, Constantine, not to be outdone by his father, built WINDY HILL nearby and sired thirteen children of his own.

A brother of Constantine, William Temple, would later raise the log walls of his home, BRENTVALE FARM, across the way but could manage only seven Sneed offspring.

When the youngest of the clan, Alexander Ewing, grew to manhood, he got the family tradition back on the track again by building FOXVIEW around 1835 and matching his father and oldest brother in offspring output with twelve more little Sneeds.

That it took only four wives to bear their four husbands forty-four children in a day and time when death in childbirth always lurked just around the corner can hardly be considered less than a miracle. Certainly, it is proof that the Sneed women were made out of the same hardy stuff as the men they married.

With us now and still in a perfect state of preservation after almost a century and a half, FOXVIEW boasts this same sturdy character. More classical in concept than the other Sneed houses of Old Smyrna Road, its white-pillared entrance portico and delicately laced balustrade give FOXVIEW a very distinct Greek Revival flavor all its own.

110

FORGE SEAT
1808
The best way to lose an argument

The late afternoon sun has a way of draping a shawl of golden mellowness over the ancient brick shoulders of FORGE SEAT.

If this old house seems to have been with us forever, it almost has. Built in 1808 by a hard-muscled man who hammered things out of iron, FORGE SEAT gives the distinct feeling that it remains in our midst today out of a quietly subtle, creaking determination all its own. Perhaps this old place is sustained by the same kind of special pride that prompted its builder and first master, Sam Crockett III, to turn out the best long rifle ever forged in frontier Middle Tennessee.

Like the spring rains that sweep across these Cumberland foothills, reputations had a way of traveling fast in those days; one of the quickest ways to lose an argument was to get caught dead in the sights of a Sam Crockett rifle. No single backwoods soul ever looked any harder for the very best way to deal with hostile Indians and British regulars than did Andrew Jackson. Some say that Old Hickory, himself, on his way to the Creek War in the fall of 1813, stopped off at FORGE SEAT just long enough to arm his Tennessee Volunteers with some of these coveted weapons.

Collector's treasures today of extreme rarity, each of these FORGE SEAT rifles had cut into its barrel the initials "S. & A. C."—proof enough that Sam's son, Andrew Crockett, worked with his father as a gunsmith in the nearby little log cabin forge that gave his old house its unique and colorful name.

With its poplar wainscoting, delicately turned stair spindles, and heavy ashen floors—all rubbed smooth and warm by the traipsing of many years across its threshold—FORGE SEAT, perhaps more than once, offered its hospitality to that vagabond Tennessee kinsman, Davy Crockett, one day destined to die in glory, killing Santa Ana's Mexicans on the walls of the Alamo.

111

CENTURY OAK
Circa 1845
Hoofprints on the stairs

Hazard Wilson II made no bones about it: Samuel, the oldest of his eight sons, was far and away his favorite boy.

When Samuel married Lucy Ann Marshall in 1845, Mr. Wilson proved to be just as straightforward with his pocketbook as with his tongue. His wedding present to the young couple was an elegant three-storied brick house on Wilson Pike. Boasting a twin brace of handsomely parapeted chimneys, toasted warm in winter by twelve yawning fireplaces and crowned with a third floor grand ballroom, the original CENTURY OAK was considerably finer even than the family's own ancestral home, RAVENWOOD.

Samuel's death in 1851, at the early age of twenty-eight, paved the way for a younger brother, Franklin, to take Lucy Ann Wilson's hand in marriage two years later and become the second master of CENTURY OAK.

Wrapped in the sackcloth of a most unusual phenomenon, tragedy called again on the Wilson household on a hot June day in 1856, when a mother's intuition forecast the death of still another of her sons.

Emmeline Wilson was attending a social function at CENTURY OAK, when she suddenly demanded that her carriage must be brought around immediately. Doubtless, the other guests were shocked into a fan-fluttering tizzy by Mrs. Wilson's insistence that there was bad trouble at RAVENWOOD. Her fears would be borne out in just a matter of moments. Hardly more than halfway home, she learned that her deaf and dumb fourteen-year-old boy, Walter, had just been killed by an accidental shotgun blast at almost the precise instant of her strange premonition.

To a born and bred Middle Tennessean like Frank Wilson, a horse thief and a bad batch of sour mash whiskey were facts of life to be avoided. When the Civil War overflowed a stream of horse-hunting Yankee marauders down Wilson Pike, the time had come for drastic action. Despite the tedious journey up three flights of stairs, CENTURY OAK'S grand ballroom, on more than one occasion, served as the secret hiding place for a number of Frank Wilson's finest thoroughbreds.

Although the grand ballroom is gone now—ripped away by a fierce windstorm that struck this old place in 1904, Frank Wilson's unique ingenuity in turning it into a wartime stable will always be a part of CENTURY OAK'S colorful heritage.

Just as the Yankees had sought to deprive Frank Wilson of his thoroughbreds and the elements had cost CENTURY OAK its three-storied grandeur, the onward march of progress would bring along its own bitter pills. Situated originally in a grove of ancient oaks and first known as OAK HALL, this fine old house stood helplessly by the wayside when the railroad huffed and puffed this way in 1912. Even though the railroad would knock down more than a score of its lordly trees and usher in another age, CENTURY OAK has always preferred to remain untouched by it all—to listen forever for the faint sound of hoofbeats on the grand stairway of its romantic past.

112

RAVENWOOD

1825

". . . the Midas touch . . ."

James Hazard Wilson II once claimed he could make money chained to a rock. Before the ill winds of Appomattox swept him from the pinnacle of success, this Middle Tennessee baron of big business could count a net worth of nearly $2,000,000 in slaves, deep south plantations, and Mississippi River steamboats.

If James Hazard Wilson learned early how to please his purse, there was only one woman who could ever please his heart. On March 21, 1825, with Sam Houston at his side as best man, this young Tennessee blade with the Midas touch would take his own thirteen-year-old first cousin, Emeline Wilson, as his bride for a lifetime.

Together, some four years later Emeline and James Hazard Wilson would raise for themselves a fine marble-manteled house on Wilson Pike. Just as his early Indian friends had once called Sam Houston "The Raven," so would the Wilsons' new home be named RAVENWOOD in his honor.

As with so many of these old places RAVENWOOD would know its share of the triumphs and tragedies of life in early Middle Tennessee. It can recall with joy the first cries of nine Wilson children born beneath its roof. It also can remember with a special kind of sorrow a seemingly endless stream of bitter tears. They began in 1851 when James Hazard Wilson's favorite son, twenty-eight-year-old Samuel, suddenly passed away at nearby CENTURY OAK. An only daughter, little Emeline, and two more Wilson brothers would follow Samuel to the family burial plot within the next three years. The broken heart of RAVENWOOD'S household had barely begun to mend when tragedy lifted its latchstring again in 1856. In a freak accident, deaf and dumb young Walter Wilson had been shot to death on the front veranda of his home by a falling gun he had just leaned against the stairway in RAVENWOOD'S entrance hall.

If the brief span of but five years had cost James Hazard Wilson the lives of four sons and a daughter, it was the death of his beloved wife, Emeline, in January, 1860, that finally broke the 'bloody but unbowed' spirit of the first master of RAVENWOOD.

As if this saga of sorrow had not been enough for one lifetime to endure, the Civil War would sweep away most of James Hazard Wilson's great fortune and leave this man with the Midas touch to sleep forever in the eternal indignity of an unmarked grave somewhere alongside Wilson Pike.

HOOKERHILLS
Circa 1829
An inch as good as a mile

The oldest portion of this picturesque house was built by a hot-headed Irishman whose pre-Civil War feud with a brother spilled over into the present century.

HOOKERHILLS had its beginning around 1829 when Samuel R. Shannon hacked out the logs of a two story double-house on a piece of land furnished by his father, old George Shannon, whose earliest days in these parts leaned all the way back to 1784.

In what turned out to be an unhappy circumstance for years to come, Sam's brother, James, also carved his homesite out of a nearby piece of Shannon ground.

The bad blood between Sam and James started to flow sometime before the Civil War. It centered around just exactly how a certain county road was to run through their adjoining tracts. Coveting every inch of ground as only two iron-jawed Irishmen can, neither Sam nor James would give an inch, and the disputed road was forced to twist and wind along their fence lines right on down into the 20'th Century. As bad blood between brothers often will, it oozed down into succeeding generations so that neither the feud nor the road could be straightened out until both pieces of property finally passed from the hands of the Shannon heirs.

If one of Middle Tennessee's most famous family feuds lends HOOKERHILLS a particular aura all its own, the passing years have bestowed a special warmth and mellow charm on this old place.

The present day visitor to HOOKERHILLS will be entranced by its quaint little tea room and antique shop on the grounds nearby. Its name? You guessed it: The Tenant House.

114

TRAVELLERS' REST
1799-1812-1821
A fat man's joke and a cold cannonball

Historic TRAVELLERS' REST in Nashville was the home of Judge John Overton, an early roommate of Andrew Jackson and one of the best friends Old Hickory ever had.

Built in three stages that spanned two decades, TRAVELLERS' REST, proudly owned today by The National Society of the Colonial Dames of America in Tennessee, represents one of the Volunteer State's most painstaking and rewarding restorations.

If ever a house reflected the temperament and character of the man who built it, such a house is TRAVELLERS' REST. Unlike his good friend, the flamboyant Jackson, John Overton had looked to the feet of hard work and patience to carry him to the pinnacle of wealth and influence in the Old Southwest of his day. By the time the election year of 1824 rolled around, without frill or fanfare to mark his rise, Judge Overton was the undisputed leader of the famous "Nashville Junto" that had thrown Old Hickory's hat into the presidential ring against Clay and Adams. More than once, this distinguished group of William B. Lewis, Felix Grundy, Sam Houston and John Henry Eaton would meet with the Judge in his library at TRAVELLERS' REST to plot the strategy that would one day open the doors of the White House to Andrew Jackson of Tennessee.

Four years earlier, this diminutive, self-effacing son of the old frontier had become the fifty-four-year-old bridegroom of the widow, Mrs. Mary McConnell White May. Shortly after their marriage, TRAVELLERS' REST got four new rooms and became the house that hosted the notorious Peggy Eaton in its parlor in 1830, dined seven Confederate generals at its table during the Civil War and saw the final, futile hour of the Battle of Nashville fought out among the stark naked December branches of its Peach Orchard.

Years later rotund William Howard Taft of Ohio, then a federal judge, paid a visit to TRAVELLERS' REST, pointed to the Confederate "Stars and Bars" on the wall and asked of Mrs. John Overton, Jr., "What flag is that, Madam?" Mrs. Overton was quick to reply: "The flag of my country, Sir!" On Taft's way out later in the evening, his hostess had handed him a cannonball that had been picked up in the Peach Orchard. "You sent it to us hot," she smiled. "I return it to you cold."

Open to the public today by The National Society of the Colonial Dames of America in Tennessee, John Overton's TRAVELLERS' REST will live long among the most cherished relics of historic Middle Tennessee.

BELLE MEADE
1853
Queen of the Cumberland hills

Nashville's BELLE MEADE plantation bridges a special stream in early Middle Tennessee history. It can remember when a father had to make his tomorrow by the sweat of his brow, while his son's tomorrow seemed to be guaranteed forever.

For John Harding the first BELLE MEADE was 250 acres of stubborn stumps and a dogtrot log cabin on the top end of the old Natchez Trace. In the field of such a humble beginning as this, the seeds of magnificent BELLE MEADE were planted as early as 1807, the year John Harding bought Dunham's Station. Daniel Dunham and most of his family had died here fighting Indians on the banks of Richland Creek no more than fifteen years before.

With an obvious knack for acquiring land and putting it to the plow point at a profit, John Harding eventually moved his family from their dogtrot home to a fine

The square pillars of BELLE MEADE still bear the scars of a bygone day when the Civil War came storming across its rolling acres.

Nothing can compare with the aura of fall at BELLE MEADE.

Early pioneer cabin of John Harding still stands today as a highlight of any visit to the grounds of BELLE MEADE.

new brick house nearby. By 1852, when this second BELLE MEADE was gutted by fire, the reins of running the plantation were in the younger hands of a son, William Giles Harding, the man who built the BELLE MEADE we know today.

Some say that the great architect, William Strickland, who conceived the State Capitol and the famous Presbyterian Church in downtown Nashville, designed this grand Greek Revival house shortly before his death, April 6, 1854. Family tradition, however, gives credit for the planning of the present BELLE MEADE to William Giles Harding and his many-talented second wife, the former Elizabeth Irwin McGavock. It was this same enterprising and gracious daughter of old Randal McGavock of CARNTON who had taken over the management of the plantation during the Civil War when her husband, a general in the state militia, was arrested by the Federals as a political prisoner and "ardent secessionist." It has been estimated that Gen. Harding had earlier donated some $500,000 toward the defense of his native Tennessee.

During the first year of the Union Army's occupation of Nashville, the toll taken on BELLE MEADE'S smokehouse and stables was disastrous. On the General's eventual release and return home, he filed for $32,000 in damages with the Federal Board of Claims, but there is no record of restitution ever being made.

For two weeks preceding the Battle of Nashville, BELLE MEADE was the headquarters of one of Gen. Nathan Bedford Forrest's division commanders, James R. Chalmers. The great square limestone pillars of this old place still bear the pockmarks of bullets from a skirmish fought on its front lawn at the opening of the battle. A daughter of the house, Miss Selene Harding, is said to have bravely stood on BELLE MEADE'S steps during the hottest part of the fight waving her handkerchief in encouragement to Gen. Chalmers' hard pressed Southerners.

William Giles Harding was never one to put all of the eggs of his prosperity in one basket. This proved to be the salvation of BELLE MEADE in the years that followed the War. If freeing the slaves had dethroned King Cotton and left most of his contemporaries land poor and destitute, good management and diversification enabled Gen. Harding and his new son-in-law, William H. Jackson, to rebuild BELLE MEADE into a model plantation again. For another half century to come fine herds of sleek Aldernay

The famous carriage house and stables are landmarks of BELLE MEADE'S past glories.

Pres. Grover Cleveland and his White House bride spent a portion of their honeymoon as guests in these twin bedchambers.

Entrance hall and grand stairway.

BELLE MEADE'S dining room has hosted
such distinguished guests as Presidents
Cleveland and Taft.

cattle, Cotswold sheep and Cashmere goats would graze its fabled acres alongside some of the choicest purebred horseflesh to be found anywhere in the world. During this period the "Belle Meade Stud" and stables became a legend in their own time. Behind the long reach of its endless stone fences pranced such proud champions as Iroquois, until 1954 the only American-bred winner of the English Derby at Epsom Downs; Luke Blackburn, the Citation of his day; Bonnie Scotland and his son, Bramble, and others too numerous to name.

Although the bulk of Gen. Harding's long and colorful life was devoted to developing the finest thoroughbreds ever to set hoof to the turf of his time, he owned no portion of a gambler's heart. One of the General's first resolves was ". . . never to bet a cent on the result of any contest of speed or any game of chance."

BELLE MEADE and its twenty-four acres of Old South charm and matchless natural beauty are maintained and opened to the public the year around by the Association for the Preservation of Tennessee Antiquities, a non-profit organization dedicated to the restoration of historic heirlooms in the Volunteer State.

Some of the grandest balls in
Tennessee history have been
staged in the parlors of
BELLE MEADE.

Sitting room at BELLE MEADE.

BATTLE OF NASHVILLE
1864
Three strikes and you're out

If ever a general had a knack for fighting the wrong battles, it was John Bell Hood, commander of the Confederate Army of Tennessee. At Atlanta he had lost the city to Sherman. At Franklin he had lost his temper and more high ranking officers ever killed before or since in a single fight. At Nashville this gallant, ill-fated Texan lost the South's final glimmer of hope.

For the two weeks that followed the slaughter at Franklin, Gen. Hood had strung what was left of the Army of Tennessee like a frayed shoestring across the hills just south of Nashville. Although his hungry men, half frozen in their thin line of rifle pits, were outnumbered more than two to one, he was still itching for a fight.

On the fog-blanketed morning of Dec. 15, at six o'clock sharp, Gen. George H. Thomas, "The Rock of Chickamauga," granted Hood his wish. When he hit both flanks and the center of the Southern line like a blue steel sledgehammer, the Army of Tennessee was forced to hang on by its fingernails. At one point during the first day's fighting an isolated Rebel artillery unit of 148 men managed to hold a division of 4,000 Yankees at bay for two full hours before Hood had to fall back and form a new defense line.

The next day was a disaster for the Confederates. Around four in the afternoon, after repeated assaults by the determined Federals, Hood's left flank folded like a sheet of paper. Once his center caved in, the Civil War witnessed the one and only time a Southern army fled the field in rout and confusion. A number of the victorious Yankees were so amazed at such a sight that they dropped their rifles to clap their hands in elation and disbelief.

With Hood's retreat from Nashville the last flame of hope for the Confederacy in the West flickered faintly for a moment and then went out forever.

BELMONT
1850
Biscuits full of secrets

When Isaac Franklin died in 1846, he left his young wife one of the richest women in the United States.

Although bereaved at the loss of a husband old enough to be her father, Adelicia Franklin was not one to linger long in her widow's weeds. After waiting a polite three years, the vivacious Mrs. Franklin became the bride of Col. Joseph A. S. Acklen of Nashville. Shortly after their marriage, the Acklens engaged a distinguished Italian architect to build them a Renaissance villa like no other in Tennessee's capital city.

When completed in 1850, BELMONT was nothing less than a world unto itself. Its one hundred and eighty acres boasted Old World gardens of misty marble fountains, fine statuary from every corner of Europe and an ever blooming abundance of flowers and bulbs for every season. All could be viewed in the shade of five handsomely ornate cast iron summerhouses appropriately placed at vantage points about the grounds. To wave this wand of floral majesty across its gardens, BELMONT had its own long ranks of greenhouses and a watering system considered nothing less than miraculous for its day. During the Civil War its hundred and five foot water tower was used more than once as a signal post by the Union Army.

BELMONT'S zoo, featuring all sorts of birds and animals, proved a constant delight for the children of the Acklen's countless friends, while its art gallery was acclaimed the most magnificent private collection in the entire South. Many of its finest paintings and etchings were gathered by Mrs. Acklen on her numerous visits to the Continent.

An ardent horsewoman of much renown, Adelicia Acklen was an intimate friend

Grand stairway at
BELMONT.

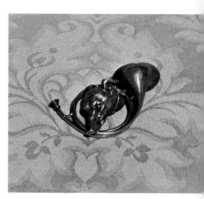

This Horn and Hound's Head
pin was a personal gift to
Adelicia Acklen from a
distinguished European
friend—the Empress Eugenie of
France, another noted
horsewoman of her day.

of France's Empress Eugenie, also a devoted patron of the hunt. Well able to afford the friendship of royalty, Mrs. Acklen once paid $5,000 for the dress she wore when introduced at the English Court of St. James.

As might be expected, BELMONT was as extravagantly lavish in concept and proportion as its grounds. No expense was too large and no detail was small enough to be overlooked in the creation of this uniquely Greek Revival flavored Italian villa. Unbelievably enormous, both inside and out, BELMONT once housed two pianos and two organs in the double drawing rooms on either side of its grand entrance hall. For the recreation of Mr. Acklen's gentleman friends, BELMONT boasted billiard rooms and its own bowling alley. To host the gay cotillions and elegant soirees of that day, there was the Atrium or huge ballroom with magnificent pier mirrors that reached almost to the frescoing of its handsomely vaulted ceiling.

China used by Adelicia Acklen during
her reign as the illustrious first
mistress of BELMONT.

In the years before the Civil War
BELMONT is said to have boasted the
finest art collection in the entire
South. Even today gentle babes sleep
on here in the quiet peacefulness of
eternal marble.

121

Although the Union Army held Nashville almost the entire length of the Civil War and Federal officers were often guests at BELMONT, there could never be any doubt where Adelicia Acklen's true sympathies lay. Mrs. Oscar Noel, Sr., a granddaughter, recalls an ingenious method developed by Mrs. Acklen for getting military information through the Federal lines to Confederate headquarters. Her communiques were written on tiny slips of paper and carefully baked inside a bucket of thick, fluffy biscuits. These biscuits and her ten-year-old son, Joseph, perched innocently on the back of an old gray mule, would then ride past unsuspecting Yankee sentries on a mission of mercy to a needy Negro family on the other side of town.

BELMONT was incorporated as a part of Nashville's Ward-Belmont College in 1890, when the house and grounds were purchased from the estate of colorful Adelicia Acklen—a Middle Tennessee belle who had ridden to the sound of the horn with an empress and kissed the hand of Britain's grandest queen.

*Jenny Lind, the famous "Swedish Nightingale,"
was accompanied by this piano during her
celebrated concert visit to Nashville in 1851.*

BELAIR

1838

Death came too soon

Fall visits BELAIR in a blaze of glory and carefully spreads a flaming blanket of red and gold across its lawn.

By the time of his daughter Elizabeth's marriage to Joseph Clay of Kentucky, John Harding—the founding father of BELLE MEADE PLANTATION—was well established in the front ranks of Middle Tennessee's landed gentry. Out of a generous heart and befitting a man of his circumstance, he deeded Elizabeth and his new son-in-law a tract of 1,000 Davidson County acres upon which to build their home and plant the fields of a promising future.

All too soon, however, the untimely death of Joseph Clay would leave the ambitious beginnings of BELAIR to be completed by a young Virginian and his wife, William and Julia Lytle Nichol.

Exactly when BELAIR was begun by the Clays lies eclipsed in the scrapbook of the past. Its completion date can be put at 1838, since this was the year the grand stairway and one story wings were added by the Nichols. The double-decked Greek Revival entrance and sprawling verandas strung between these low resting wings make BELAIR a distinctive Middle Tennessee manor house with Lower Gulf Coast leanings toward a traditional love of outdoor leisure living.

To manicure the final charm of BELAIR, a Scotsman, one Daniel McIntyre, was imported from across the far Atlantic to tend the greenhouse and formal garden of hyacinths, buttercups and ever glorious lilies-of-the-valley. Walled off from the rest of the world of that day by fence rows of golden honeysuckle and crepe myrtles, the triangular and symmetrical plantings of BELAIR'S formal garden are said to have been remarkably similar to those of Mrs. Jackson at THE HERMITAGE.

TWO RIVERS
Circa 1859
". . . the halls of yesteryear . . ."

Stacked two stories tall and proud of every inch, TWO RIVERS was built by David H. McGavock just before the Civil War.

The site chosen for this magnificent manor house came under the hand of David McGavock through his wife, Willie Harding, a daughter of Nashville's historic BELLE MEADE plantation. Obviously an offspring of that place in time when a well-to-do southern gentleman could still afford to feed his hunger for elegant pretension, TWO RIVERS was probably completed around 1859.

William Harding, Mrs. McGavock's distinguished father, is credited with naming this old place, so long a landmark of the gently rolling hills between the Cumberland and Stones River.

The first house to be built on these picturesque heights—a two story brick affair with a distinct pioneer flavor—may have been here as early as 1802. Still clinging to life in the sturdy tradition of its humble beginnings, this early Middle Tennessee hearthstone bridges the gap between the "Age of Necessity" and the "Age of Affluence" in the Old South's antebellum era.

Staring back at the world beyond its handsome garden of ancient boxwoods, the TWO RIVERS of David and Willie Harding McGavock is a massive and proud house that seems to dwarf everything about it. Even the golden glory of its trees that blaze across its rolling lawns each and every fall seems to pay homage to this regal old monarch of the distant past.

Owned and maintained today by the City of Nashville, TWO RIVERS, now opened to the public, beckons to all who come its way to take time out for a visit and a journey through the halls of yesteryear.

THE HERMITAGE
1819-1831-1835
Her every wish—a general's command

For more than a century and a half Andrew Jackson has remained uneclipsed as Tennessee's most famous son. Child veteran of the Revolution, orphaned yokel from the Waxhaws, leather-pounding frontier jurist, erstwhile dealer in fine horses and black men, a framer of his state's first constitution, Congressman, Senator, cockfighting gambler and hotheaded duelist, Major-General of Militia, crusher of the Creek Nation, consort of pirates and rogues, "Hero of the Battle of New Orleans," conqueror and Governor of the Florida Territory, ardent suitor, adoring husband, doting father, and, finally, seventh President of the United States—all of these and much more was Andrew Jackson. If others of his time stood tall, this man was a giant of his age. If others accomplished much, Andrew Jackson moved the mountains of an era. Small wonder today that his beloved home, THE HERMITAGE, visited by tens of thousands annually, lingers ever on as the Volunteer State's most venerated hearthstone.

Fortunately, THE HERMITAGE has gone almost untouched by the hands of time since that June day, 1845, when Andrew Jackson drew his last breath on this earth. Perhaps, as the old warrior lay dying, the last and deepest regret of his life may well have been that his dear Rachel was not spared long enough to share with him the white-pillared glory of his great "mansion house" as we know it today.

Though Rachel Jackson was not destined to enjoy THE HERMITAGE in its present grandeur, could she but stroll these shade-strewn acres once again, perhaps her dark eyes would turn first to the far northeast corner of its grounds. Here stand the final remains of that little cluster of log cabins that had always, somehow, claimed her heart.

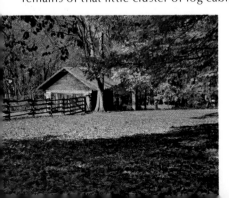

Old log building moved from the Jacksons' previous home, HUNTER'S HILL. Split rail fence is typical of early Middle Tennessee.

125

The fallen leaves of November gather quietly about this downspout receptacle of the house Pres. Jackson had rebuilt after the second HERMITAGE was struck by the disastrous fire of 1834.

Beneath the gentle arc of this dome Andrew Jackson of Tennessee finally lay down to rest forever at the side of his beloved Rachel.

To this very spot Andrew had brought her in 1804 after financial reserves had forced the sale of their second home, HUNTER'S HILL. In what was then a two story blockhouse, flanked by three humble one room cabins, she and Andrew had fitted their hands together in the glove of a new beginning and had lived out fifteen of the happiest and most eventful years of their lives.

It was to this first HERMITAGE that Andrew Jackson was brought that May morning in 1806—an ounce of lead from Charles Dickinson's dueling pistol lodged near the fierce heart that would tolerate no shadow to fall on Rachel's good name. It was also to this first HERMITAGE that the wily Aaron Burr came the following summer, seeking once again to entice Andrew with his cloudy dreams of western empire beyond the Mississippi. Fortunately, however, before he had contributed little more than a nod or two of his shaggy head, the keen nose of Jackson's backwoods intuition had sniffed out the faint scent of treason. Otherwise, he may well have become a part and parcel of the ex-Vice-President's ill-fated schemes, for there was one common thread that could have bound these two men together—ambition. For the one, his yearnings would lead to disgrace, exile, and oblivion; for the other to fame, fortune, and a fine new brick house for Rachel Jackson.

The War of 1812 began the snowball of events that rolled Andrew Jackson out of the shadows of obscurity and into the limelight of national prominence. If he had begun his public life as a circuit riding frontier lawyer, his road to real glory would take him first across the log breastworks of Horseshoe Bend where, March 27, 1814,

Near the Jackson's Tomb are found the graves of other members of the family.

Both God and man have joined hands to create the fall fantasy of Andrew and Rachel Jackson's HERMITAGE, as seen through the archway of its present day museum.

he and his Tennessee Volunteers bathed the Tallapoosa River countryside of Alabama in the blood of 800 Creek braves.

That fall, with the grateful thanks of the whole southern frontier still ringing in his ears, Andrew Jackson turned toward New Orleans. Here—in the swamps of Chalmette—with a rag tag conglomeration of sharpshooting backwoodsmen, a sprinkling of friendly Indians, the 7th U. S. Infantry, and Jean Lafitte's motley mob of Baratarian pirates, he smashed the 6,000 man army of British General Sir Edward Pakenham. On this January 8th day, 1815, Jackson had swapped fifty-eight wounded and thirteen dead for 2,037 British casualties and had sent the noble Sir Edward home to England, his body pickled in a barrel of West Indies rum. With the events of this same day, in the swamps of Chalmette, Andrew Jackson had planted his feet firmly on the path to the White House.

If New Orleans had brought more fame than fortune, a rising cotton market and three straight bumper crops at THE HERMITAGE soon took care of that. Alas, the orphan from the Waxhaws had become a man of substance to be reckoned with. Only a second expedition to Florida against the Seminoles in the spring of 1818 now stood in the way of making Rachel the mistress of a suitable manor house at THE HERMITAGE.

That following autumn, racked with chronic dysentery and further sickened with disgust at Washington's weak-kneed criticism of his Florida policies, Andrew Jackson came home to lick his wounded pride and hang up his battle sword for the last time. Broken in body, if not in spirit, he was now more determined than ever that work begin on "Mrs. Jackson's new house" before the year was out, even though he was convinced he would never live to move with Rachel from their two story log house of nearly fifteen years.

"Mrs. Jackson's new house," though not elegant in the Tidewater sense, was of brick and commodious enough to stretch some eighty-five feet across its southerly front

To an Andrew Jackson home from the wars, even the first HERMITAGE must have been a most welcome sight.

127

and house two floors of at least four large rooms each. From a small entrance porch, a central hall, dividing the two front parlors, ran the full depth of the house. Behind the parlor on the right was the master bed chamber. Directly across the hall and adjoining the second parlor was a spacious dining room. The upstairs was given over entirely to sleeping quarters, one of which may have been used by the Jacksons' adopted son, Andrew, Jr.

A second of these upstairs bedrooms was occupied by that vagabond artist, Ralph E. W. Earl. The widowed husband of one of Rachel's many nieces, Earl would spend seventeen years under the Jackson roof, painting portraits of the family and other prominent Middle Tennessee gentry of that day. As Rachel Jackson's protege, young Earl had waiting at his brush tips commissions from the great and near-great alike, so imposing and unending was the stream of guests that poured across the threshold of the 1819 HERMITAGE. Among some of the most frequent visitors were men like Sam Houston, a handsome, ramrod of a young lawyer to whom the General had taken a special shine and who, like Jackson, was a child of destiny in his own right. There was also Judge John Overton, almost a life-long friend who could recall those unhappy days when Rachel had belonged first to the insanely jealous Lewis Robards. Frequent callers, too, were Tennessee's beloved Governor McMinn and Senator John Henry Eaton, backwoods pal and future Secretary of War whose choice of a bride would one day shake up a whole presidential cabinet. Finally, with the visit of President James Monroe in the summer of 1819, THE HERMITAGE entertained its most distinguished guest of all. Six years hence, as a U. S. Senator, Jackson would throw open wide the doors of THE HERMITAGE to welcome another old warhorse, the great Lafayette.

In the spring before Monroe's visit, the General had hired a full-fledged English gardener William Frost, to design and landscape the grounds of THE HERMITAGE. Under Frost's direction, a gracefully winding cedar-lined drive found its way up to the house's southerly entrance. To the east, laid out in wending walkways and flower beds of formal symmetry, was the ever-blooming world of "Mrs. Jackson's garden." A constant lover of all things beautiful on this earth, Rachel Jackson was particularly fond of this spot. Ever in tune to his wife's every fancy, at her death in 1828, on the eve of Jackson's first inauguration, he laid his beloved Rachel to rest in a far corner of this east garden.

Three years later, Andrew Jackson, Jr.'s marriage to Sarah York of Philadelphia was the occasion for an 1831 face-lifting at THE HERMITAGE. Among the changes made at this time were the addition of a new kitchen and smokehouse at the rear, along with a two story back veranda of rather elegant proportions. The dining room was enlarged into a banquet hall that would accommodate as many as 100 guests, and hitched to the east and west walls were the one story wings that have become an architectural trademark of the present day HERMITAGE. The front portico, stretching between these wings, though increased to a more imposing demeanor, still sheltered only the ground floor level after the '31 remodeling was completed.

In 1834, during Jackson's second term in the White House, to all of his other troubles in guiding the ship of state was added the tragic news that THE HERMITAGE had been all but demolished by a flash fire that October.

Only the walls and part of the banquet hall were usable in the restoration which Jackson had begun almost immediately and which was completed in 1835, as the great white-pillared HERMITAGE we know today.

His frail shoulders stooped a little more, his purse pinched dangerously thin by the then formidable $6,500 rebuilding cost and additional refurnishing expenditures, Jackson returned to THE HERMITAGE in 1837. Here he would once again make his way out of the doldrums of financial adversity and live out the final eight years of his life.

Since coming into the hands of The Ladies' Hermitage Association, April 5, 1889, Andrew Jackson's house and grounds have known the same tender care he always bestowed on his beloved Rachel, the constant devotion he always offered his country, and the enduring love that always turned his footsteps ever toward THE HERMITAGE.

Like Andrew Jackson—true worth asks little and gives much.

TULIP GROVE
1836
Only six months to live

No trip to THE HERMITAGE is complete without a visit to TULIP GROVE, the home of Andrew Jackson Donelson—Old Hickory's favorite nephew and namesake.

Distinguished in history as Jackson's executive secretary for two terms in the Presidency, Andrew Jackson Donelson completed TULIP GROVE in the summer of 1836 as a belated wedding present to his first wife.

If radiantly beautiful Emily Donelson had reigned for most of seven years as her uncle's official White House hostess, her tenure as mistress of TULIP GROVE would not be nearly so long. Six months after moving into her new Tennessee home, Jack Donelson's beloved red-haired Emily was destined to die of tuberculosis at twenty-nine—just two days before her husband's arrival from Washington for the Christmas holidays.

Christened first POPLAR GROVE and later renamed at the suggestion of Pres. Van Buren, TULIP GROVE'S Greek Revival perfection is the handiwork of master artisans Joseph Reiff and William Hume, the same pair that rebuilt THE HERMITAGE after the fire of 1834. Boasting some 140,000 bricks in its regal walls, it is unbelievable, even for that day and time, that such a magnificent house could be completed from top to bottom for a total outlay of only six thousand two hundred and fifty dollars. Of this amount, Old Hickory himself is said to have chipped in at least a third for the carpentry work and laying of the bricks.

Just as Andrew Jackson Donelson's first wife, Emily, had also been his first cousin, so a second cousin, Elizabeth Martin Randolph, in 1841, became his second wife. The new Mrs. Donelson, the widow of a grandson of Thomas Jefferson, was at her husband's side when Pres. Tyler appointed him charge d'affaires to the Republic of Texas in 1844. After figuring prominently in the Lone Star State's entrance into the Union, Donelson later spent three years in Berlin as Polk's Minister to Prussia.

Ever a man to hover close to the elbow of his convictions, 1856 saw Jack Donelson run unsuccessfully for Vice President on the Know-Nothing ticket with Fillmore. This final act of his public life had cost him the ire of friend and family alike back home in Tennessee, and in 1858 Andrew Jackson and Elizabeth Donelson sold TULIP GROVE and turned their backs forever on these Cumberland foothills.

Today, the home of this distinguished Tennessee son is perfectly preserved and graciously opened by The Ladies' Hermitage Association to all who come to walk in the shadow of a man who served his country under three Presidents with a special loyalty and quiet devotion all his own.

Rachel Jackson never lived to see the little chapel her husband built to her memory on the lawns of TULIP GROVE.

FAIRVUE
1832-1839
". . . I like this house . . ."

By the time he was forty-three, the slave trade and a Midas touch had made Isaac Franklin the most eligible bachelor in all of Sumner County. After brief service in the War of 1812, this handsome son of the Old Southwest had dealt in "black ivory" all the way from Virginia to New Orleans and laid the cornerstone of a fortune. By 1832 he could well afford to build a house like FAIRVUE on a two thousand acre Middle Tennessee estate and don the more respectable mantle of a well-to-do planter.

If Isaac Franklin was the kind of man who knew what he wanted and had what it took to get it, he would soon meet his match in beautiful Adelicia Hayes of Nashville.

While on an 1838 visit in the Gallatin home of Judge and Mrs. J. J. White, twenty-one-year-old Adelicia and the Whites decided to pay an afternoon social call on the bachelor baron of FAIRVUE. Arriving unannounced and failing to find Mr. Franklin at home, Adelicia had signed his guest book in a most unusual way: "Adelicia Hayes, Nashville, Tenn.—I like this house, and I set my cap for its master."

The next year, 1839, saw Adelicia Hayes become Mrs. Isaac Franklin, the first mistress of FAIRVUE and the bride of a man old enough to be her father.

Shortly after their marriage had lifted every prominent eyebrow in Davidson and Sumner County, the size of FAIRVUE was almost doubled when Spanish architects from New Orleans added a second story above the kitchen and enclosed the south wing's colonnade with seven new rooms.

At his death in 1846, Mr. Franklin owned six hundred slaves and seven plantations that comprised more than ten thousand acres of prime farmlands in Louisiana and Tennessee.

Like an oversized mushroom the "spring house" at FAIRVUE is a source of constant wonderment.

FAIRVUE'S rear entrance.

Isaac Franklin's will, though it left Adelicia one of the richest young widows in the country, also provided that should she remarry FAIRVUE was to become a school for young boys. Following her second marriage three years later to Col. J.A.S. Acklen of Nashville, the enterprising Adelicia, however, managed to retain title to FAIRVUE until 1882 when she sold the house and grounds to two New Yorkers, Mr. and Mrs. Charles Reed.

The new owners of FAIRVUE were as colorful as they were wealthy. Mr. Reed, christened Charles Weed at birth, had changed his name when his family had seen fit to disown him for his blockade running activities to the Confederacy during the Civil War. Mrs. Reed, once a lady in waiting to Queen Victoria, had also been disavowed by her family for becoming the bride of the notorious Charles Reed.

Early in life this native New Yorker had developed a strong addiction to the scent of fine horseflesh and the red roses of the winner's circle. Once his feet were planted firmly in the bluegrass bosom of Sumner County, Mr. Reed soon busied himself turning FAIRVUE into the finest stud farm of his day. While Mrs. Reed amused herself by strolling about her garden, dressed in a Mother Hubbard and smoking black cheroots, the mid-1880's found visitors from every corner of the nation hastening to FAIRVUE to purchase some of this country's finest thoroughbreds. Once when his good friend and fellow New Yorker, August Belmont, offered him $60,000 for a prime mare named Thora, Mr. Reed had replied indignantly, "Sir, that amount of money wouldn't buy enough hair out of her tail to make a fiddle bow!"

Some years later, at Mr. Belmont's death, Charles Reed had appeared at the dispersal sale of the Belmont stables with $110,000 in I.O.U.'s from his late friend. Out of generosity to the Belmont family, when the bidding for St. Blaise, a recent winner of the English Derby, reached $10,000, Mr. Reed suddenly jumped the bid to the outlandish total of Mr. Belmont's notes, tore up the I.O.U.'s and returned to Tennessee with St. Blaise.

Never one to stoop to half measures, once when Mr. Reed had been unable to locate a hammer in one of his stables, he had amazed every hardware dealer in Gallatin by sending to town for a wagonload of hammers. On another occasion he had turned five thousand homing pigeons loose on the grounds of FAIRVUE and watched them scatter to the four winds without the return of so much as a single bird. It seems that the man who had sold Mr. Reed the pigeons

Front parlor and portrait of Isaac Franklin, builder of FAIRVUE.

Dining room at FAIRVUE.

The passage of time has wrought little havoc at FAIRVUE. The portrait of its first mistress still has a place of honor in its parlors.

failed to mention that there was only one female in the whole flock.

By 1908, like his pigeons, Charles Reed's once vast fortune had taken flight. The Reeds were soon forced to sell their beloved FAIRVUE and turn their backs forever on its satin upholstered ethereal world of plush and plenty.

For a time, at least, FAIRVUE would regain some small measure of its past prestige when the Grasslands International Steeplechase was held here in the early Depression years of 1929 through 1931. With an initiation fee of $30,000 and annual dues of $10,000, the Grasslands Association listed among its limited membership men of such mountainous means as John Hay Whitney, William duPont and yeast king, Julius Fleischmann.

Following the demise of the Grasslands Association, a new and unexpected blessing came FAIRVUE'S way in 1934. In that year the house and grounds were thankfully purchased by Mr. William Wemyss, a co-founder of the huge Genesco shoe corporation. From March to November, 1939, Mr. and Mrs. Wemyss brought about the miraculous restoration of a grand old house that would soon have been torn from the pages of history had they not come this way when they did.

One visit to FAIRVUE'S grand entrance hall was all it took for beautiful Adelicia Hayes of Nashville to decide to set her cap for the master of this house.

OAKLAND
1835
A President's physician

The great Andrew Jackson was no stranger to Sumner County's OAKLAND. Racked and ruined by too many hard campaigns, Old Hickory more than once brought his many ailments here to be treated by his good friend Dr. Daniel Wade Mentlo, its first lord and master.

Pure Georgian in design and graced by a handsome Greek Revival entrance portico, OAKLAND was built for Dr. Mentlo in 1835 by John Fonville, the same master artisan who designed and constructed GREENFIELD and the NATHAN HARSH HOUSE, just to the eastward on State Highway 25.

As was typical of that day and time, the bricks for OAKLAND'S outside and inside walls were fired on the place, while all of its framing and foundation materials sprang from the sweet sod of the good Doctor's endless acres. Among the few necessities that had to be imported were the solid brass doorknobs and locks from Carpenter & Sons of Birmingham, England.

Among OAKLAND'S most prized possessions today is the little frame medical office of Dr. Mentlo, situated humbly near the entrance gate to this old place's immediate grounds. Doubtless, many was the time in this very building this kind and able physician ministered to the aches and pains of the seventh President of the United States and one of our greatest Americans.

The aches and pains of a President were often listened to within these humble walls.

135

JAMESON-HARSH HOUSE
1832
Three of a kind

The JAMESON-HARSH HOUSE was never intended to wave the flag of frill or pretense. Though boasting ten spacious rooms, each with its own fireplace, there is an air of simple dignity and warm hospitality in the humble Georgian demeanor of this fine old Sumner County home.

Built for the James B. Jameson family in 1832 by master craftsman John Fonville, the JAMESON-HARSH HOUSE is one in a trilogy of Georgian gems Fonville erected in this section of Middle Tennessee during the Thirties. Like children sired by the same father, there are certain marked similarities to be found in GREENFIELD, OAKLAND and the JAMESON-HARSH HOUSE. Each claims the traditional rear story ell, the same simply pitched roof and the classic grace of a first floor Greek Revival portico that breaks the severity of the otherwise pure Tidewater Georgian facade.

While all three of these houses share these same common traits, each seems to have its own distinct personality, as if borrowed from the different generations that have lived in and loved them through the years.

CASTALIAN SPRINGS

1828

The largest of its kind

CASTALIAN SPRINGS—or WYNNEWOOD as it is known today—may well be the largest log house ever built in the State of Tennessee. One hundred and forty-two feet from end to end, this unique old place was literally hacked out of the virgin forests of a wilderness frontier by the ambitious axes of three young men—Alfred R. Wynne, Stephen Roberts and William Cage.

Conceived originally as a wayside inn for weary travellers between Hartsville and Gallatin, CASTALIAN SPRINGS hovers on a hill above Bledsoe's Lick, an ancient sulphur spring where hordes of buffalo once gathered in such numbers its discoverer, Isaac Bledsoe, was afraid to leave his horse for fear of being trampled to death. Built on a tract of land owned by Alfred Wynne's wife, the former Almira Winchester of nearby CRAGFONT, CASTALIAN SPRINGS became the Wynne family's home in 1834, after it had failed dismally as a pioneer hostelry.

As a son-in-law of Gen. James Winchester and a close friend of Andrew Jackson, Alfred Wynne shared the belief of these two old frontier pine knots that failure was only a temporary circumstance for a man with the courage of his convictions. Col. Wynne never gave up the idea of paying guests at CASTALIAN SPRINGS, and by the 1840's he had built this fourteen-room log house into the most exclusive mineral water resort in the state. Catering to the planter-rich gentry of his day, the Colonel strung a row of log guest cottages across the east lawn of his home, complete with servants' quarters, an ever bountiful smokehouse and doctor's office of its own. Soon, even famous Bledsoe's Lick came to be known by the more aristocratic and high-sounding name of Castalian Springs. For visitors like Andrew Jackson, much more intrigued by the scent of fine horseflesh than sulphur water, the Lick Creek track in the nearby bottom was an added drawing card.

Even though the Civil War marched to and fro across the long-leaning shadow of CASTALIAN SPRINGS, this old place remained untouched by it all, as if Yank and Reb alike were reluctant to disturb the peace and tranquility of this earthly Heaven.

Even in the setting sun of a life that lacked just seven years of spanning a whole century, hosts of guests continued to be welcomed to CASTALIAN SPRINGS by Col. Wynne, a courtly and generous man who had turned a dream into a reality for the enjoyment of generations.

Appropriately, the main house and grounds—now known as WYNNEWOOD— remained in the hands of the Colonel's descendants until 1971, when they were deeded to the State of Tennessee to be ever preserved and cherished as one of its most historic sites.

CRAGFONT
1802
Castle in the wilderness

CRAGFONT is a house that will take your breath away. Built in the shape of The Cross and chiseled out of stone to last forever, there is no other old home like this in all of Tennessee.

With a brawny-shouldered kind of grace and beauty all its own, CRAGFONT was conceived in the vibrant vitals of the Old Southwest, nurtured by its virgin forests and delivered out of the womb of its Cumberland quarries as the proud guardian and ruling magistate of every hill and valley it surveys.

If CRAGFONT is no ordinary house, its builder, Gen. James Winchester was no ordinary man. Promoted in the field for conspicuous bravery during the Revolution, this native son of Maryland saw service under both Washington and Greene, was twice captured by the British and witnessed the surrender of Lord Cornwallis at Yorktown. At the war's end he moved to the fledgling Cumberland settlement of Bledsoe's Lick in 1785. Two years later he was chosen as one of three commissioners charged with the founding of Sumner County, then a part of North Carolina. Just prior to his appointment as brigadier general of the old Mero District, Winchester's brother, George, was killed by the Indians during one of their frequent raids on the tiny settlement hovered around the Lick.

Tennessee's admission to the Union in 1796 found Gen. Winchester, not only a member of the state's first Senate but presiding as its first Speaker. Some two years hence he began raising the thick stone walls of CRAGFONT, the grand Federal house above Bledsoe's Lick it would take him four long years to finish.

In building a totally complete home like CRAGFONT, Gen. Winchester made the transition from pioneer log cabin to magnificent manor house in one fell swoop. CRAGFONT did not evolve through a series of additions and afterthoughts but was

The southwest bedroom of CRAGFONT is proof enough that James Winchester never forgot the comforts of his native Maryland.

The stenciling of CRAGFONT'S mantels is a craft long lost to the artistry and patience of yesteryear. Both are still found in abundance in this hardy old Middle Tennessee house.

born outright from start to finish to resemble and compete favorably with the finest of the country estates of the General's Tidewater heritage.

The War of 1812 had turned James Winchester's back on his great stone house on the hill to again answer his country's call. After a temporary eclipse for his defeat at River Raisen, the end of hostilities would find him in command of the Mobile area under his good friend and frontier sidekick, Andrew Jackson.

The General's last public service came in 1819 as a commissioner in the running of the Chickasaw boundary between Mississippi and Tennessee. It was during this period that he, Jackson and Judge John Overton founded the city of Memphis and Winchester saw his son, Marcus Brutus, become its first mayor. Ever a student of the classics, two other sons in the General's brood of fourteen children bore names like Lucilius and Valerius Publicola.

Gen. Winchester died at CRAGFONT on July 26, 1826, in the same month as two other great Americans, John Adams and Thomas Jefferson—the country's second and third President. Thirty-eight years later, at the end of a life that spanned from Indian massacres and the birth of this nation to the Civil War that tore it to pieces, Mrs. Winchester was buried at her husband's side beneath the long falling shadow of the grand old house they had shared together and loved so well.

CRAGFONT stands today in all its Stoic splendor, perfectly restored and open to the public under the auspices of the Sumner County Chapter of the Association for the Preservation of Tennessee Antiquities.

Sitting room at CRAGFONT, where the worth of a friend was often measured by the speed of her knitting needles, not to mention a few dropped stitches of gossip about a neighbor down the road.

There is a delicate flavor about CRAGFONT'S
dining room that has welcomed guests to
the generous table of this old place
for generations.

There can be little doubt that the nursery at
CRAGFONT was one of the busiest rooms in
this house, since General and Mrs.
Winchester saw to the birth of some
fourteen children.

James Winchester's office hosted the likes of
Andrew Jackson and John Overton. Together
this hard-knuckled triumvirate of pioneer
sons would found the city of Memphis.

CRAGFONT'S old kitchen is still strong with
the savor of yesterday's hams and the
hard-bricked determination to stay with
us forever.

IN RUTHERFORD
COUNTY

OAKLANDS
1820's—1850's
No hot meals on Sunday

OAKLANDS is an old Murfreesboro house made famous by a hard-charging ex-slave trader named Nathan Bedford Forrest.

At 4:30 on the morning of July 13, 1862, Gen. Forrest and a pack of his Rebel-yelling troopers galloped out of the darkness and up to OAKLANDS to capture a sleepy-eyed Col. W. W. Duffield and a detachment of his Seventh Michigan Cavalry. Shortly after noon, in this same house, Forrest accepted the surrender of all of Murfreesboro by the Federals. This formality aside, the master of OAKLANDS, Dr. James Maney, invited men of both sides to dine together across the table of temporary friendship in his grand banquet room.

For a month Col. Duffield would be a guest in OAKLANDS' household, recovering from wounds received in Forrest's raid. To ice the cake of his hospitality to a former enemy, Dr. Maney even invited Mrs. Duffield down from Detroit to be with her husband. In 1866 the Duffields expressed their gratitude with a handsome silver service, a collection of books for the good Doctor's library and a fine assortment of rare Meerschaum pipes.

OAKLANDS, draped in a shawl of Middle Tennessee snow, would host another distinguished visitor with the arrival of President Jefferson Davis the following December. Accompanied by Gen. Robert E. Lee's son—Gen. George W. C. Lee—Davis had come south from Richmond to make a personal inspection of Bragg's winter line along Stones River. During his stay at OAKLANDS, the President was a guest in the room directly over Dr. Maney's library, and Gen. Bragg was quartered nearby in the room above the parlor. Other notables to enjoy the hospitality of the Maney household were the great oceanographer, Matthew Fontaine Maury; the Hon. John Bell, who had opposed Lincoln on the Constitutional Union ticket in 1860; and Leonidas Polk, "Bishop-General of the Confederacy."

With much of the flavor of an Old World Italian villa, the oldest portion of OAKLANDS dates back to the 1820's and the early arrival of Dr. and Mrs. James Maney from their native North Carolina. As a highly respected physician in Murfreesboro for many years, Dr. Maney was also such a good Presbyterian that during his lifetime no hot meals were ever cooked at OAKLANDS on Sunday.

Handsomely furnished today and restored to its rightful perfection by the Oaklands Association, this old place—now open to the public—is visited by thousands annually as one of Middle Tennessee's most historic antebellum hearthstones.

141

SAM DAVIS HOME
1810-1855
"If I had a thousand lives . . ."

Sam Davis of Tennessee may well be called "The Nathan Hale of the Confederacy." His boyhood home in Rutherford County near Smyrna is visited by thousands annually. From both sides of the Mason-Dixon Line they come to pay their respects to the memory of a young Rebel soldier who chose the end of a hangman's rope rather than betray his country.

If Sam Davis no more than crossed the threshold of manhood before he stood on the trapdoor to eternity, his kind of courage and devotion to duty have immortalized him forever in the hearts of his fellowmen.

Although there are no photographs or portraits to tell us what Sam Davis looked like, what he did in the last week of his life on Earth has become a living legend—chiseled in stone, praised by poets and written indelibly on the pages of history.

In the wake of Fort Sumter, Sam Davis was among the first to answer his country's call. As an eighteen-year-old cadet at Nashville's Western Military Institute, early May saw him enlist as a private in the First Tennessee Volunteer Infantry. In the span of less than twelve months, Sam's regiment would follow four of the Confederacy's greatest generals into battle. The First Tennessee got its baptism of fire at Cheat Mountain, Va., in Robert E. Lee's very first campaign of the War. Two months later it would serve in the foot-deep snow of the Shenandoah Valley and along the Potomac with the great Stonewall Jackson. The fall of Fort Henry and Fort Donelson brought the First Tennessee back West in the spring in time to do battle under Johnston and Beauregard at Shiloh, where Sam was slightly wounded. With Bragg in Kentucky, he would be wounded again at Perryville the following October.

Just thirteen months later, as a courier in Coleman's Scouts, Sam Davis was captured near Minor Hill, Tenn., by two Kansas "Jayhawkers" from Union Gen. Dodge's Sixteenth Corps encamped around Pulaski. Hidden in Sam's boots and under his saddle on this

These old slave cabins figured in the restoration of the SAM DAVIS HOME.

Side porch and a fall visit at the SAM DAVIS HOME.

fateful Friday, Nov. 20, 1863, were the intricately detailed plans of all Federal fortifications in Middle Tennessee. In his saddlebags were ". . . three wash balls of soap . . ." and three toothbrushes for Gen. Bragg. Also found on him at the time was a letter of introduction to Bragg's headquarters and a pass through the Confederate lines signed by "Captain E. Coleman."

As it turned out, "Coleman" was actually the fictitious name of Capt. Henry B. Shaw, Sam's commanding officer and the man Gen. Dodge was really after as leader of Rebel scouts in Middle Tennessee. Captured shortly after Sam, Capt. Shaw was thrown into the same jail in Pulaski without the Federals ever suspecting his true identity. To keep this secret, Sam Davis would pay with his life.

So precisely accurate was Sam's information for Bragg that Gen. Dodge immediately became suspicious of a high level leak in Union Army headquarters in Nashville. When both threats and offers of leniency failed to pry loose Sam's tongue, the General, caught in the double dilemma of admiration and frustration, called a court-martial to try Sam Davis as a spy. That this young Tennessee soldier was wearing the uniform and sidearms of a Confederate scout when captured seemed to make no difference in the espionage charges brought against him. A few hours of one-sided testimony and Sam's continued refusal to tell what he knew was all it took for a conviction and a sentence of death by hanging. Exactly one week after falling into enemy hands, Sam Davis was scheduled to die at the end of a Yankee rope on Pulaski's Seminary Hill. The night before his execution, he sat writing by candlelight in his prison cell:

"Pulaski, Giles County, Tenn., Nov. 26, 1863

"Dear Mother: O how painful it is to write you! I have got to die to-morrow—to be hanged by the Federals. Mother, do not grieve for me. I must bid you good-bye forevermore. Mother, I do not fear to die. Give my love to all.

Your dear son . . ."

Dining room.

143

Sam announced his arrival on his last visit home by tapping gently on one of the windows in the family room.

Sisters' room.

The next morning Sam rode out to the scaffold on Seminary Hill, seated astride his own coffin. Along the way more than one Union officer begged him to save himself by telling Gen. Dodge what he wanted to know. From time to time the same plea came from among the thousands of men of the Sixteenth Corps who gathered to witness this sad event. To a messenger with a last appeal from Gen. Dodge's headquarters, Sam Davis gave his final answer: "If I had a thousand lives to live I would give them all gladly rather than to betray a friend or my country."

Today, Sam Davis sleeps ever so peacefully in the little family burial plot at the rear of his childhood home. The handsome shaft of Italian marble, placed above his grave in 1866, tells the story of this heroic young Tennessean in words of simple devotion:

> ". . . He Laid Down His Life for His Country.
> A Truer Soldier, a Purer Patriot, a Braver Man
> Never Lived. He Suffered Death on the Gibbet
> Rather than Betray His Friends and Country."

No old house in Middle Tennessee has quite the same aura of nostalgia as the SAM DAVIS HOME on picturesque Stewart's Creek. The front or oldest portion of the house dates back to 1810. Raised out of logs, this section was covered over with poplar siding by Sam's father, Charles L. Davis, when he built the rear addition in 1855.

Perfectly preserved and administered today by the Sam Davis Memorial Association, the entire 168 acre complex represents a typical pre-Civil War, upper middle class Rutherford County plantation. At the rear of the house is the conventional unattached kitchen and the ever present smokehouse. Flanked on one side by the overseer's office and a humble row of empty slave cabins, the SAM DAVIS HOME and grounds were purchased from the Davis family by the State of Tennessee in 1927 and are open to the public the year around.

One of the distinct charms of this old place is that it is furnished with many of the pieces that were in the house when Sam Davis grew up here. There are even some of his own personal belongings such as his bootjack and the old trunk that went off with him to Western Military Institute just before the War. Of special interest is the Family Room and the two rocking chairs in which Mr. and Mrs. Davis may have been sitting when Sam suddenly tapped on the window that November night of his last visit home. Just outside is the giant rock where, later that night, Sam had untied his horse, waved a final goodbye and galloped off on his journey into eternity.

Sam's final resting place.